The Kylemore Abbey Cookbook

THE KYLEMORE ABBEY COOKBOOK

EDITOR
MARY DOWLING

GILL & MACMILLAN

Gill & Macmillan Ltd
Hume Avenue, Park West
Dublin 12
with associated companies throughout the world
www.gillmacmillan.ie
© Kylemore Abbey 1997
978 07171 2540 1

Index compiled by
Helen Litton

Design and print origination by
O'K Graphic Design, Dublin

Colour reproduction by
Typeform Repro Ltd, Dublin

Printed by
ColourBooks Ltd, Dublin

This book is typeset in 11/14 pt Cochin.

The paper used in this book is made from the wood pulp of managed forests.
For every tree felled, at least one tree is planted, thereby renewing natural resources.

A catalogue record for this book is available from the British Library.

13 15 14 12

CONTENTS

Contents

Contents

FOREWORD

I t gives us great pleasure to write this Foreword for *The Kylemore Abbey Cookbook*.

For many years we have enjoyed the culinary expertise of the Nuns of Kylemore, in the dining-room and also in the restaurant. It is wonderful to get the real taste of home-produced and home-cooked food, lovingly prepared.

Undoubtedly, the recipes in this book are presented, tried and tested with the same loving care.

We wish the project every success.

Archbishop Walton and Louie Empey

PREFACE

Another cookbook! What can this collection of recipes have to offer that is different? As you will see, the recipes presented here come from the kitchens of a Monastery. This, of course, may provoke another question. Why do these Nuns seem so very concerned about the stove and table? Surely a simple and abstemious lifestyle would preclude a serious and deep preoccupation with the good things of life? Not so! The Judaean-Christian attitude to all creation is one of a healthy respect and appreciation. In the earliest book of the Bible, Genesis itself, we find the writer presenting God Himself contemplating the work of His hands with deep satisfaction — God saw that it was good. This is the touchstone for our appreciation, and in the New Testament we meet Christ, on numerous occasions, sharing meals with His followers and enjoying feasts and celebrations where good food played a central role.

The scene of the first Christian miracle, for example, is the wedding feast of Cana, where such excellent wine was miraculously provided to save embarrassment to the young couple. The multiplication of the loaves and fishes shows that Christ had cared that His followers be given a nutritious meal — with plenty to spare. He would eat at the house of Simon, and be ready to defend the gentility of Magdalene, who washed His feet with her tears and anointed them with precious ointment. At Bethany, Martha was so busy preparing good food, He would chide her gently that she should query her sister's preference for listening to His word.

The most famous prayer of all in the Christian tradition — the 'Our Father' — has a central plea that we might be granted 'our daily bread'.

The paschal meal of the Jewish tradition was to serve as source and setting for the Christian Eucharist — the great Meal of Thanksgiving.

It ought, then, to come as no surprise that when St Benedict of Norcia wrote his Rule (A.D. 580), he should set great store by the kitchen, the refectory and the needs of the monastics. Good food is God's gift to us, and the sharing of that food creates community. The holy Abbot could think of no worse punishment than that a refractory monk be excluded from the common table — taking his meals alone! That is how sensitive he was to the potential of a shared meal.

ACKNOWLEDGMENTS

✠

PAX

The Benedictine Nuns at Kylemore Abbey
extend the 'Pax' — Peace of St Benedict — to all their readers.

The Abbess, Mother Clare Morley O.S.B., and Community would like to express warm gratitude to all who have so generously contributed to *The Kylemore Abbey Cookbook*. Without the culinary wisdom and practical expertise of many people, this book would never have been written:

To Mary Dowling, our good friend, whose knowledge and skill is reflected in the careful planning and preparation of the project.

To Dom Paul McDonnell for sharing the secrets of his 'beachcombing' expeditions and the breadth of his liturgical experience.

To our wonderful staff who have carefully researched and painstakingly tested each recipe, lest there be a hint of 'pinch and fist'!

The Abbess would like to say a word of thanks to those members of the Community, particularly Sister Benedict and Sister Bernard, who brought to this cookbook flavours old and new, and all others who shared their recipes and who are individually credited throughout the pages.

Thanks must also be given to Kate O'Connor, Phyl O'Kelly, Paula Daly, BIM, An Bord Bia, Don Carlos, Don Roberts and Guy Williams, for their help and advice along the way.

Finally, a special thank-you to Eveleen Coyle for her direction and enthusiasm.

Thank you one and all.

HISTORY OF KYLEMORE ABBEY

✣

The history of the Benedictine Community of Nuns, now resident at Kylemore Abbey, has its beginnings a long way back, to the year 1665. At that time Irish and English women were joining religious communities on the continent as a result of the dissolution of the monasteries in the British Isles. In 1665 the Bishop of Ypres, a small town in Belgium, invited Dame Marina Beaumont, a Benedictine Nun living in an Abbey in Ghent, to establish a Benedictine Abbey in the town. Fifteen years later, in 1680, the first Irish Abbess was elected and this saw the beginning of the 'Irish Dames of Ypres'.

Five years later in 1685, King James II, the last Catholic King of England, who was a patron of the Irish Dames of Ypres, built a convent in Dublin and invited the Nuns to come and live there. However, following the Battle of the Boyne, James was forced to flee for his life. So just four years after their arrival in Ireland the Community had no choice but to return to the Abbey at Ypres.

Fortunately, the Abbess of the day, Lady Josephine Butler, had had the foresight to hold on to the Ypres house. Upon their return to Ypres the Nuns experienced a reversal of fortune and, to say the least, fell on very hard times. Food was scarce; herb tea and beans constituted the staple diet of the Nuns for several years. Thankfully, faith and perseverance won through and brought renewed prosperity to the Community. By the early 1900s, Community records show that 'the garden produced abundant fruit and vegetables, and the Community was adequately fed' — but not for long. In 1914 the Nuns were bombed out of their home during the Battle for Ypres. They fled to London, and then to the safety of Oulton Abbey. Eventually they made their way back to Ireland and settled in Macmine Castle in County Wexford, where they stayed until 1920. In that year the nuns purchased, with the help of public loans, the beautiful property of Kylemore

Mitchell Henry (second from the left at the back), the original owner of Kylemore Castle

Auctioneer's sign for Kylemore Castle, dated 1902

The magnificent vaulted ceiling of the Gothic Church

The President, Mary Robinson, with Mother Clare and Sister Magdalena, when she re-opened the Gothic Church in 1994, after the extensive restoration

Detail of the carved stonework in
the restored Gothic Church

Castle. A classic mansion in an area of unsurpassed beauty, it was built in 1868 by Mitchell Henry, surgeon and financier, as a gift for his wife.

The house was in bad repair, but the Nuns, with the faith and perseverance which had sustained them through many trials, set about making it their home. They established a girls' boarding school, which still thrives today, and a guest house to cater for the many fishermen who came to enjoy the sport on the river and lake. The farm supplied much of their needs — dairy produce, meat and poultry — while salmon and trout came from the lake.

Life was not to be easy, however. Tragedy struck again in 1959, when a bad fire destroyed almost two-thirds of the castle. The Nuns set about the Trojan task of rebuilding their home, and in due course the school was reopened and expanded.

With the advent of tourism development in the West of Ireland in the 1980s, this unique area saw the beginnings of a sustainable future. The Nuns opened a small tea room, craft shop and pottery. Over recent years these have prospered and expanded with the addition of an exhibition in the Abbey reception rooms and the restoration of the Gothic Church. The revenue generated will, it is hoped, permit further restoration and preserve this precious heritage for the benefit of present and future generations of Irish people and visitors from all over the world.

The magnificent Gothic Church in the grounds, which was in a state of decay and disintegration, was restored to its former splendour and reopened in April 1994 by President Mary Robinson. It is now a venue for prayer, reflection and recitals.

We were pleased and humbled to be awarded the 1995 AIB National Heritage Award for helping to make a better Ireland, as well as the Western Region Architectural Award for 1996 by the RIAI (Royal Institute of Architects of Ireland).

Now we are embarking on the next phase, the restoration of our eight-acre Victorian walled garden.

Sister Benedict O.S.B.

'Then are they truly monks, if they live by the labour of their hands'

Rule of St Benedict

Chapter 48

SOUPS AND BROTHS

❖

*A*ll year round, since earliest times, soup has figured on the Monastery menu. Great pots of broth, simmering gently on the kitchen range, were a permanent feature. In them, a variety of fresh seasonal vegetables cooked to succulence in rich beef or mutton broth and thickened, sometimes, by the addition of pearl barley or oatmeal. Today, the emphasis has shifted from broth to thick, or puréed, vegetable soups.

In the Kylemore Abbey Restaurant, many visitors choose a lunch of creamy vegetable soup, wheaten bread, Irish cheddar cheese and home-made chutney. The flavour of the soup changes every day, but it is always full of 'today's vegetables, today'. Depending on the cook's ingredients, the final flavour is always a surprise.

NOTE: *All soups yield 4–6 portions, depending on whether you serve it as a starter or a main meal. Butter is specified for the most part, but use margarine if you prefer.*

STOCK

The basis of all good soups is a good home-made stock, and the result is well worth the time and effort. The water in which meat is cooked is an excellent base for soup. If the stockpot is a little too much trouble these days, it is a good idea to get bones from the butcher, with a piece of leg beef, or neck of mutton, and simmer for a few hours, freeze and use as needed for soups, gravies and sauces.

White Mutton Stock

1.8 kg/4 lb mutton bones
4.6 litres/8 pints/20 cups water
bouquet garni (parsley, thyme, bay leaf)

2 sticks of celery, trimmed, washed and sliced
1 carrot, peeled and chopped
1 onion, peeled and chopped

Rinse the bones and put into a large saucepan with the water. Bring to the boil, skim and add the bouquet garni. Simmer for 2 hours. Add the chopped vegetables and continue to simmer over a low heat, with the lid on, for an additional 1½ hours. Skim occasionally, remove from the heat, strain, cool, cover and store in a fridge or freezer until required. Always remember to date containers.

Beef Stock

225 g/½ lb shin beef

1.8 kg/4 lb beef bones

4.6 litres/8 pints/20 cups water

bouquet garni

a little dripping *or* fat

1 carrot, peeled and chopped

1 onion, peeled and chopped

1 tomato, sliced

Rinse the bones and dry, place in a roasting pan in a hot oven (220°C/425°F/Gas 7) to brown. Cut the meat into small pieces, and place together with the bones in a large saucepan. Add the water and the bouquet garni, bring to the boil and simmer gently for 2–3 hours. Strain. Heat the fat in a large saucepan, add the carrot and onion and fry until nicely browned, add the strained stock, bouquet garni and tomato. Simmer for a further hour. Allow to cool, then skim and strain. Refrigerate or freeze until needed. Always remember to date containers.

POTATO AND SPRING ONION SOUP

ễ▲

45 g/1½ oz/3 tbsp butter

170 g/6 oz/1½ cups spring onions, peeled and chopped

1 clove of garlic, peeled and crushed

450 g/1 lb potatoes, peeled and roughly diced

bouquet garni (parsley, thyme, bay leaf)

1.2 litres/2 pints/5 cups good white stock

salt and pepper

150 ml/¼ pint/⅔ cup cream

chopped parsley

Melt the butter in a large saucepan, add the onions and the garlic and sauté gently for 5 minutes; do not allow them to colour. Add the potatoes and continue to cook for a further 10 minutes. Add the bouquet garni, stock and seasoning and simmer for 40 minutes. Remove from the heat, take out the

Kylemore Abbey in its classic setting, overlooking the lake

Mother Clare with Sister Jarlath
and Mother Mary, former Abbess

bouquet garni and blend the soup at low speed to a smooth purée. Check the seasoning, add the cream, reheat but do not boil. Sprinkle with the chopped parsley before serving.

The following soups can be made using the basic recipe for
Potato and Spring Onion Soup:

Potato and Smoked Salmon Soup

Add little strips of smoked salmon to the finished soup; trimmings are fine for this purpose. As well as being very tasty, the salmon adds a touch of elegance for a special occasion.

Potato and Smoked Haddock Soup

Place 170 g/6 oz smoked haddock in a saucepan, barely cover with milk, bring to simmering point and simmer for about 3 minutes. Remove the saucepan from the heat, strain off the milk and break the fish into bite-sized pieces. Add the fish to the potato soup with a little of the strained milk. This is a substantial soup and is ideal as a hearty luncheon dish.

Potato and Crispy Bacon Soup

Cut 3 rashers into very small pieces and fry gently in a little butter until crisp and golden brown. Add to the finished potato soup just before serving.

Potato and Fresh Herb Soup

When making the soup, add extra parsley stalks which can be removed before blending. Finally, when the soup is ready, add a generous amount of chopped parsley, thyme leaves, chopped chives and indeed any fresh herbs you particularly like and have to hand.

CURRIED PARSNIP SOUP

ॐ

55 g/2 oz/4 tbsp butter	2 medium parsnips, peeled and sliced
1 medium onion, peeled and chopped	1 tbsp flour
	1 rounded tsp curry powder

1.2 litres/2 pints/5 cups good stock
salt and pepper

150 ml/¼ pint/⅔ cup cream
chopped chives *or* parsley to
garnish

Melt the butter in a large saucepan, add the onion and parsnips, cook over a gentle heat, with the lid on, for about 10 minutes. Add the flour and the curry powder, mix well and cook for 1–2 minutes. Then add the stock and simmer gently for a further 30 minutes. Blend the soup at low speed to a smooth purée; check the seasoning. Add the cream and reheat gently. Garnish and serve.

Variations of Parsnip Soup

Parsnip and Horseradish Soup

Use the recipe above, but omit the onions and curry powder; add 1 tablespoon of horseradish relish to the finished soup.

Parsnip and Apple Soup

Omit the curry powder from above recipe. To the finished soup add 1 medium apple, peeled and cut in small dice; simmer for 1 minute before serving.

ALMOND SOUP

4 sticks of white celery
1 onion, peeled and sliced
110 g/4 oz/1¼ cups ground
 almonds
1.2 litres/2 pints/5 cups white
 stock
bouquet garni

30 g/1 oz/2 tbsp butter
30 g/1 oz/4 tbsp flour
280 ml/½ pint/1¼ cups milk
150 ml/¼ pint/⅔ cup cream
30 g/1 oz/¼ cup toasted slivered
 almonds

Trim and wash the celery, remove coarse strings with a sharp knife, and slice. Put the celery and onions into a saucepan with the ground almonds, stock and bouquet garni. Bring to the boil and simmer for ¾ hour. Remove the bouquet garni and blend soup to a smooth purée.

Rinse out the saucepan, melt the butter, add the flour and cook for a minute. Add the milk gradually whilst whisking all the time. When thickened, add the almond liquid. Bring to the boil and simmer gently for a few minutes. Just before serving add the cream and top with a little sprinkling of slivered almonds.

LENTIL SOUP

110 g/4 oz/½ cup lentils

1.2 litres/2 pints/5 cups good chicken stock

2 lean rashers, rinds removed and cut in small pieces

1 small onion, peeled and chopped

1 stick of celery, washed, trimmed and finely sliced

½ medium carrot, scraped and diced

½ courgette, washed and finely diced

2 tbsp tomato purée

salt and pepper

chopped parsley to garnish

Wash and strain the lentils. Put in a large saucepan with the stock and bring to the boil. Simmer gently for 30 minutes. Add the rashers, onion, celery and carrot to the saucepan; simmer for a further 10 minutes. Add the courgette, tomato purée, salt and pepper, and continue to simmer for 15 minutes. Sprinkle generously with the parsley and check seasoning before serving.

MIKEY'S LETTUCE SOUP

225 g/½ lb lettuce, carefully washed

45 g/1½ oz/3 tbsp butter

110 g/4 oz potatoes, peeled and roughly diced

1.2 litres/2 pints/5 cups chicken stock

yolk of 1 large egg

150 ml/¼ pint/⅔ cup cream

salt and pepper

Chop the lettuce, melt the butter in a saucepan, add the lettuce and cook gently until wilted. Add the potatoes and the chicken stock and bring to the boil. Reduce the heat and simmer until the potatoes are cooked. Liquidise the soup, return to the saucepan and gently reheat. Whisk the egg yolk

A view of the Restaurant at Kylemore Abbey

together with the cream and add to the soup, continuing to whisk. Do not boil the soup once the egg has been added. Check seasoning and serve immediately.

This recipe is invaluable in times of abundance when lettuce is often left in the soil to decay. Mikey guards against this by arriving with armfuls of lettuce from the garden.

GREEN PEA AND MINT SOUP

30 g/1 oz/2 tbsp butter

2 medium onions, peeled and chopped

1 carrot, scraped and chopped

170 g/6 oz smoked bacon *or* ham

170 g/6 oz fresh green peas *or* frozen

1 tsp mixed fresh herbs

1 tbsp chopped fresh mint

1.2 litres/2 pints/5 cups chicken *or* vegetable stock

150 ml/¼ pint/⅔ cup milk

salt and pepper

a little cream

fresh mint leaves to garnish

Melt the butter in a large saucepan, and gently cook the onion and carrot for 5–10 minutes. Cut the bacon or ham into small pieces, add to the saucepan and continue to cook for a further 2–3 minutes. Add the herbs and mint, pour in the stock, add the peas, return to boiling point and simmer gently for 30 minutes. Blend the soup to a smooth purée, return to the saucepan, add the milk, salt and pepper, and reheat. Just before serving, top up with a little cream and garnish with the fresh mint leaves.

PARSLEY SOUP

75 g/3 oz parsley

30 g/1 oz/2 tbsp butter

1 large onion, peeled and chopped

1 clove of garlic, peeled and crushed

1 medium potato, peeled and diced

1 stick of celery, washed and sliced

25 g/1 oz/3 tbsp flour

1.2 litres/2 pints/5 cups white stock

salt and pepper

150 ml/¼ pint/⅔ cup cream

Wash the parsley in cold water, dry and chop roughly, reserving some nice sprigs to garnish. Heat the butter in a large saucepan, add the onion and the garlic and cook gently without browning. Add the potatoes, parsley and celery and continue to cook for a further 5 minutes. Stir in the flour and mix well. Add the stock, bring to the boil and cook slowly for 20–25 minutes. Blend at low speed to a smooth purée. Return to the saucepan, season, add cream and reheat gently. Garnish with sprigs of parsley.

CABBAGE SOUP

&

1 small cabbage

salt

45 g/1½ oz/3 tbsp butter

1 leek, washed, trimmed and thinly sliced

1 large onion, peeled and finely chopped

3 medium potatoes, peeled and diced

1.2 litres/2 pints/5 cups chicken stock

150 ml/¼ pint/⅔ cup cream

a little freshly grated nutmeg

Remove the outer leaves of the cabbage and cut in four. Remove the hard centre and stalks and discard. Chop the cabbage finely and wash well in salted water. Melt butter in a saucepan and sauté the leek and onion for 5 minutes. Add the potatoes and cabbage and toss for a further few minutes. Add the stock, bring to the boil and cook gently for 15 minutes. The cabbage must not be over-cooked — it needs to have bite. Season, add the cream, and sprinkle with a little grated nutmeg when serving.

MUTTON BROTH

&

1 tbsp pearl barley

450 g/1 lb neck of mutton

1.2 litres/2 pints/5 cups stock *or* water

1 carrot, scraped and diced

1 stick of celery, washed, trimmed and sliced

1 slice of turnip, peeled and diced

1 leek, washed and finely diced

seasoning

chopped parsley to garnish

Wash the pearl barley and steep in cold water for 4 hours. Wipe the meat and place in a saucepan with water, bring to the boil, discard the water and cover the meat with the stock or water. Add the strained pearl barley, bring to the boil and simmer for 1 hour or until the meat is cooked, skimming frequently during cooking. Add all the diced vegetables to the broth 20 minutes or so before the meat is cooked. Remove the meat, trim off any fat or gristle, dice the lean meat and return to the broth. Season, sprinkle with parsley and serve.

Chicken or Turkey Broth

Make as for Mutton Broth, omitting the neck of mutton and using good chicken or turkey stock instead of mutton stock.

Beef Broth

Make as for Mutton Broth, using 450 g/1 lb shin beef instead of the neck of mutton.

SEAFOOD CHOWDER

30 g/1 oz/2 tbsp butter
2 slices of smoked bacon, de-rinded and cut into small pieces
2 medium onions, peeled and chopped
2 medium potatoes, peeled and diced
110 g/4 oz smoked haddock

225 g/½ lb fresh cod
575 ml/1 pint/2½ cups fish stock
1 x 396 g tin chopped tomatoes
bouquet garni
280 ml/½ pint/1¼ cups milk
salt and pepper
chopped parsley

Melt the butter in a large saucepan and lightly fry the rashers. Add the onions and potatoes, continue to cook very gently for a further 5–10 minutes, but do not brown. Skin and cube the fish, add to the pan with the stock, tomatoes and bouquet garni. Bring to the boil, reduce the heat and simmer very slowly for 15 minutes. The fish should be soft but not flaking apart. Remove the bouquet garni, and add the milk and seasoning. Reheat, sprinkle with chopped parsley and serve immediately.

MUSSEL SOUP

'You must tread very softly and have your spade at the ready. Once you see the little spurt of water coming up from the small pile of sand — and if you are fast — you can dig out a razor-fish, a bivalve with a shell like a razor handle. This is one of the rewards of stranding. Stranding is like beach-combing except that you are searching for seafood.

The best time, so they say in Connemara, is the morning after low tide, at low water, with the wind from the north. The water will be far out, and the spoils could be oysters, periwinkles, scallops, clams, and certainly wild mussels encrusting the rocks. You can reap a large harvest, and there is great satisfaction in cooking and eating the result of your labours. Mussels straight from the briny ocean retain the taste of the sea, and my favourite recipe is this one.'

Dom Paul McDonnell

Dom Paul McDonnell's Recipe for Mussels

2.5 kg/3 lb mussels	55 g/2 oz/½ cup brown flour
2 onions, peeled and chopped	575 ml/1 pint/2½ cups milk
3 cloves of garlic, peeled and chopped	salt and freshly ground black pepper
175 ml/6 fl oz/¾ cup white wine	150 ml/¼ pint/⅔ cup cream
55 g/2 oz/4 tbsp butter	1 tbsp chopped parsley

Wash the mussels under running water, scrape the shells and ensure all grit has been removed, and remove the beards. Put the mussels into a saucepan with the onions, garlic and wine. Cover and bring to the boil. When the mussels have opened, remove from the liquid, discard any mussels whose shells have not opened, and reserve liquid for later use.

Melt the butter in a large saucepan, stir in the flour and cook for 1 minute, then add the milk, stirring continuously. Strain the fish liquid and add to the saucepan; return to the boil. Reduce the heat and simmer gently over a low heat until smooth and creamy. Remove the mussels from their shells and add to the soup. Season, and add the cream. Heat well but do not boil, sprinkle with parsley and enjoy.

FISH

❧

*I*n the early days of the Abbey, fish had strong penitential associations. Meat was forbidden during the Lenten fast, Advent and Ember Days. It was usual, also, to abstain from meat on three days each week.

Herring and mackerel were available locally. Other varieties — cod, haddock and hake — came twice-weekly from Galway, transported in dripping wooden boxes. Wild salmon, abundantly available when in season, was not seen as the fine fare it is today — in fact the humble whiting would have ranked higher within the Community. And the attitude of the time to mussels, oysters and crabs, which abounded around the coast, could be summed up in the words of Jonathan Swift: 'He was a bold man that would ate an oyster.' The popularity of fish was not helped by the then methods of cooking — boiling, frying or steaming.

Availability depended on the weather, and bad weather meant no fish. The alternative was always eggs. Sister Ita, now in her 92nd year, comments: 'In those days it was good to have anything at all to eat, and choices hadn't even been heard of.' Today's variety, and imaginative methods of cooking, are in sharp contrast to those distant days.

HADDOCK CRUMBLE

❧

675 g/1½ lb fresh haddock	1 bay leaf
75 g/3 oz/6 tbsp butter	1 clove of garlic, peeled and crushed
1 medium onion, peeled and finely chopped	4 tomatoes, skinned, deseeded and chopped
225 g/½ lb mushrooms, sliced	
salt and freshly ground black pepper	110 g/4 oz/2 cups breadcrumbs, seasoned
175 ml/6 fl oz/¾ cup each of wine and water	3 tbsp finely chopped parsley

Skin the haddock and cut into cubes. Grease 4 individual ovenproof dishes and divide the haddock evenly between them. Heat 55 g/2 oz/4 tbsp of the butter in a heavy-based frying pan and sauté the onion until tender but not browned. Add the mushrooms, seasoning, wine, water, bay leaf and the garlic, and cook over a high heat until the liquid has been reduced. Add the tomatoes and check the seasoning. Remove the bay leaf and divide the mixture evenly between the 4 dishes. Cover with breadcrumbs to which you have added half the parsley. Dot with the remaining butter and bake in a preheated fairly hot oven (200°C/400°F/Gas 6) for 30 minutes. Before serving, sprinkle the remaining parsley on top.

HADDOCK WITH RED PEPPERS

675 g/1½ lb fresh haddock
3 tbsp olive oil
450 g/1 lb onions, peeled and sliced
4 tomatoes, peeled and sliced
1 tbsp freshly chopped basil

2 red peppers, deseeded and sliced in strips
salt and freshly ground black pepper
1 tbsp lemon juice
55 g/2 oz/4 tbsp butter

Skin the haddock and cut into four portions. Heat the oil and gently cook the onions until soft.

Arrange the fish in a greased flameproof dish, cover with the sautéed onion, and follow with a layer of tomatoes. Sprinkle with basil and lastly add the pepper strips. Season with freshly ground black pepper and salt, sprinkle the lemon juice on top and dot with butter.

Cover the dish and bake in a preheated moderate oven (180°C/350°F/Gas 4) for 40 minutes.

MARGUERITE'S SMOKED HADDOCK BAKE

450 g/1 lb potatoes, peeled and sliced
1 large onion, peeled and sliced
675 g/1½ lb smoked haddock cut into small pieces
1 small can sweetcorn, drained
280 ml/½ pint/1¼ cups cream
50 ml/2 fl oz/¼ cup milk

½ tsp nutmeg
1 tbsp wholegrain mustard
salt and freshly ground black pepper
55 g/2 oz/½ cup grated cheese
55 g/2 oz/1 cup breadcrumbs
30 g/1 oz/2 tbsp butter

In a well-greased ovenproof dish layer the potatoes, onion, fish and sweetcorn, ending with a layer of potatoes. Mix the cream, milk, nutmeg, mustard and seasoning, and pour over the layers. Cover with greaseproof paper and bake in a preheated moderate oven (180°C/350°F/Gas 4) for 1–1¼ hours. Mix the cheese and the breadcrumbs together with a little seasoning, and sprinkle over the dish. Dot with knobs of butter and place under a hot grill (US broiler) until nicely browned.

SMOKED FISH COBBLER

ða

170 g/6 oz/1½ cups grated cheese
velouté sauce (quantity as below)
340 g/¾ lb smoked haddock

110 g/4 oz/1 cup diced onion
8 cheese scones

Add the cheese to the velouté sauce. Cut the fish into medium-sized pieces and put with the onion into 4 small individual pie dishes. Ladle the sauce on top. Place two cheese scones on each dish and bake in a preheated oven (150°C/300°F/Gas 2) for 20 minutes.

Velouté Sauce

575 ml/1 pint/2½ cups fish stock
1 medium onion, chopped

55 g/2 oz/½ cup flour
2 tbsp vegetable oil
575 ml/1 pint/2½ cups cream

Put the fish stock into a large saucepan, bring to the boil, add the onion and cook for 1–2 minutes. Mix the oil and flour together to form a roux, and crumble into the stock, beating all the time. Cook for 2 minutes. Remove from the heat and strain the stock, add the cream and leave aside.

Cheese Scones

225 g/½ lb/2 cups flour
½ tsp cayenne pepper

30 g/1 oz/¼ cup grated cheese
55 g/2 oz/4 tbsp margarine
water

Sieve the flour into a bowl, add the cayenne pepper and the cheese, and crumble in the margarine. Mix with enough water to form a soft dough. Turn out on to a floured board and roll out to ½–¾ inch thick. Cut into scones and leave aside.

HERB FRIED COD

4 x 170 g/6 oz fillets of cod
75 g/3 oz/¾ cup flour
salt and freshly ground black
 pepper

1 tbsp freshly chopped thyme
110 g/4 oz/½ cup butter
sprigs of fresh thyme and lemon
 slices to garnish

Wash the fillets and dry them very well. Season the flour with pepper and salt, and add the fresh thyme. Toss the fish in the seasoned flour and gently shake off any excess. Heat the butter in a frying pan and fry the fish, skin side down, for 6–7 minutes, depending on thickness. When the underside is golden brown, turn and repeat. Reduce the heat under the frying pan if necessary. Transfer the fish on to kitchen paper to drain. Put on to a warm serving dish and garnish with the sprigs of fresh thyme and lemon slices. Serve with tartare sauce.

SMOKED COD WITH YOGHURT

450 g/1 lb smoked cod
2 tsp lemon juice
280 ml/½ pint/1¼ cups milk
2 x 125 g cartons natural yoghurt

55 g/2 oz/½ cup grated Cheddar
 cheese
2 eggs, beaten
salt and pepper
½ tbsp chopped chives

Cut the cod into chunks. Gently poach it in water and lemon juice for 5–8 minutes. Remove it from the water with a slotted spoon: be careful to drain off all the liquid. Put the fish into an ovenproof dish.

Mix together the milk, yoghurt and cheese. Add the eggs, seasoning and chopped chives, and pour over the cod. Place the dish in a bain marie (page 132) and bake in a preheated oven (180°C/350°F/Gas 4) for 30 minutes until set.

SALMON IN PASTRY

225 g/8 oz packet puff pastry
225 g/8 oz cooked salmon, flaked
2 hard-boiled eggs, chopped
110 g/4 oz cooked rice
1 small onion, peeled and finely
  chopped
55 g/2 oz/4 tbsp butter

2 tbsp whipped cream
salt and freshly ground black
  pepper
juice of one lemon
1 tbsp chopped parsley
1 egg, beaten

Roll out the pastry to form two rectangles, approximately 30 x 15 cm (12 x 6 inches), and lay on a greased baking sheet. Spread the salmon over half the pastry lengthwise, next layer with the eggs, rice and onion. Dot with knobs of butter and the cream, season and sprinkle with the lemon juice and parsley. Brush the edges of the pastry with a little of the beaten egg, fold over and seal. Brush over top of pastry with the remaining beaten egg, and cook in a preheated warm to moderate oven (180°C/350°F/Gas 4) for 30 minutes. Cut into neat squares when serving.

Hot or cold, this recipe is a very tasty way of using up leftover salmon.

WHOLE SALMON BAKED IN FOIL

1 whole salmon prepared — about
  3.6 kg/8 lb
salt
170 g/6 oz/¾ cup butter
fennel sprigs
parsley sprigs

3 bay leaves
2 onions, peeled and sliced
few slices of lemon
lemon and cucumber slices to
  garnish

Place a sheet of tin foil in a greased oven dish large enough to hold the salmon. Allow sufficient foil to completely wrap the salmon. Wash and dry the salmon, season with the salt and spread butter all over, and into the cavity. Put the herbs, onion and lemon into the cavity and a little around the fish. Place the salmon on the foil and wrap loosely, sealing the edges. Put into a preheated fairly hot oven (200°C/400°F/Gas 6) for 15 minutes, then lower the heat to 150°C/300°C/Gas 2 and allow to cook for approximately 40 minutes. Leave to rest for 15 minutes. Remove the skin from the salmon while still hot. Transfer to a serving dish. Serve with Hollandaise Sauce and garnish with lemon and cucumber slices.

If serving cold, leave for several hours until cool, then place in a fridge for a further 2–3 hours. Serve with a green salad and home-made mayonnaise.

Hollandaise Sauce

2 tbsp water	55 g/2 oz/4 tbsp butter
3 tbsp wine vinegar	salt and pepper
2 egg yolks	

Put the water and vinegar into a saucepan and bring to the boil. Continue to boil until reduced to 2 tbsp, then cool slightly. Put the egg yolks into a bowl, stir in the vinegar and water. Place the bowl over a saucepan of warm water and heat gently, stirring until the mixture thickens. The water in the saucepan must not be allowed to boil. Gradually whisk in the butter, in small pieces; remove from the heat if the sauce is thickening too quickly. Add seasoning and serve warm but not hot.

Mayonnaise

2 egg yolks	1 tsp caster sugar (US superfine sugar)
salt and pepper	280 ml/½ pint/1¼ cups olive oil
½ tsp mustard	1 tbsp vinegar

Put the egg yolks into a bowl with the salt, pepper, mustard and sugar, and mix well. Add the oil, drop by drop, whisking all the time. As the sauce thickens, you can add the oil a little more quickly. When all the oil has been added, thin down with the vinegar and check seasoning.

SALMON WITH CUCUMBER SAUCE

———————— ❧ ————————

55 g/2 oz/4 tbsp butter

1 small cucumber grated

55 g/2 oz/½ cup flour

425 ml/¾ pint/1¾ cups milk to
which 1 tbsp of chicken stock has
been added

1 tbsp lemon juice

425 ml/¾ pint/1¾ cups cream

salt and freshly ground black
pepper

4 salmon cutlets *or* fillets (170 g/
6 oz per person)

slice of onion ⎫
parsley stalk ⎬ to poach fish
peppercorns ⎭

Melt the butter in a pan, add half the cucumber and cook gently for 1–2
minutes. Add the flour and stir in the milk; cook slowly, whilst continuing to
stir until thickened. Remove from the heat and blend at low speed until
smooth. Add the lemon juice, the remaining grated cucumber and the cream.
Season, mix well and keep warm.

Place the salmon in a shallow pan and barely cover with water. Add the
slice of onion, parsley stalk and a few peppercorns. Put the lid on the pan
and gently poach the fish for 8–10 minutes. Remove the fish from the pan
and keep warm. Spoon the sauce on to a hot serving dish, arrange the
salmon on top, and garnish with lemon wedges.

PLAICE IN ORANGE CREAM SAUCE

———————— ❧ ————————

4 good-sized fillets of plaice

1 orange, rind and juice

175 ml/6 fl oz/¾ cup white wine

90 ml/3 fl oz/⅓ cup fish stock *or*
water

15 g/½ oz/1 tbsp butter

2 tsp cornflour

110 ml/4 fl oz/½ cup cream

salt and pepper

sprigs of parsley and orange
segments to garnish

Skin the fish and fold over the fillets. Put on to a greased ovenproof
casserole, either lidded or cover with foil. Add the orange juice and rind, the
wine, the stock, and dot with knobs of butter. Cover and bake for 15 minutes
in a preheated moderate oven (180°C/350°F/Gas 4). Remove the casserole
from the oven and strain the liquid into a small saucepan. Place the fish on

Sister Anna fishing

The Gothic Church
set against the
rocky hillside

a serving dish and keep warm. Blend the cornflour with the water, add to the fish liquid and cook for 2 minutes, stirring. Add the cream, reheat the sauce, check seasoning, and pour the sauce over the fish. Garnish with parsley and orange segments.

STUFFED PLAICE

4 whole medium-sized plaice, gutted and cleaned

Stuffing

55 g/2 oz/4 tbsp butter

1 small onion, peeled and finely chopped

1 clove of garlic, peeled and crushed

110 g/4 oz/½ cup cooked rice

½ red pepper, peeled, deseeded and cut into very small dice

170 g/6 oz mushrooms, wiped and sliced

½ medium carrot, scraped and shredded

salt and freshly ground black pepper

sprigs of parsley and lemon wedges to serve

Heat the butter in a saucepan and sauté the onion and garlic for 2 minutes. Add all the other ingredients and sauté for a further 2 minutes; season. Remove the stuffing from the saucepan and allow to cool.

Wash and dry the prepared fish. Lay flat on a board. With a sharp knife, make an incision down the centre of the bone. Fillet the fish from each side of the bone to form a pocket.

Place the stuffing into the fish pockets. Dot the fish with butter and place in a greased ovenproof dish. Cover with foil and bake in a preheated moderate oven (180°C/350°F/Gas 4) for 20 minutes. Garnish with the parsley and wedges of lemon.

SOLE IN CIDER SAUCE

4 good-sized fillets of sole

1 spring onion, finely chopped

1 bay leaf

salt and freshly ground black pepper

175 ml/6 fl oz/¾ cup cider

90 ml/3 fl oz/⅓ cup water

sprigs of parsley and wedges of lemon to garnish

Cider Sauce

20 g/¾ oz/1½ tbsp butter

20 g/¾ oz/3 tbsp flour

sufficient cream to make up to
280 ml/½ pint/1¼ cups when
added to reserved fish stock

Skin the fillets and lay them on a greased ovenproof dish. Add the onion and bay leaf and season. Pour the cider and water over the fish, cover the dish and cook in a preheated fairly hot oven (200°C/400°F/Gas 6) for 10–15 minutes. Remove the bay leaf, pour off the liquid and reserve. Keep the fish warm.

Melt the butter in a saucepan, add the flour and cook for 1 minute. Gently pour in the fish stock and cream, cook slowly and stir continuously until the sauce has reached the consistency of cream.

Arrange the fish on a warm serving dish, pour the sauce over and around the fish, and garnish with lemon wedges and sprigs of parsley.

SKATE ON FRIDAY

Life as a medical student in turn-of-the-century Dublin is the subject of *Tumbling in the Hay*. The Hay Hotel (so called because the window boxes were stuffed with hay for the cabbies' horses) was run by Stephen and Maria, once in the employ of Gogarty's father. They provided refreshment for night owls and a welcoming haven for students and other vagrants. Maria and Stephen dish up the hospitality amid scenes of comic chaos and Rabelaisian delight. The atmosphere belongs to the Middle Ages.

'It was the long table (at the end of a long passage) full of boiling coffee, hot tripe and onions, skate (on Fridays) and crubeens that attracted the weary nightfarer.'

Tumbling in the Hay, Oliver St John Gogarty

4 skate wings

55 g/2 oz/4 tbsp butter
salt and pepper

Bouillon

1 chopped onion

1 chopped carrot

a sprig each of parsley and thyme

1.5 litres/2½ pints/6 cups water

salt and pepper

Make the bouillon by putting all the ingredients in a large saucepan and bringing to the boil. Simmer for 30 minutes. Put the skate wings into the saucepan and poach for 10–15 minutes. Lift out the skate and place on a warmed dish. Melt the butter, add the salt and pepper, and pour over the fish.

Serves four.

By kind permission of Oliver D. Gogarty

OYSTERS À LA MORNAY

30 g/l oz/¼ cup grated Parmesan cheese

¼ tsp French mustard

150 ml/¼ pint/⅔ cup white sauce

1 tbsp cream

salt and white pepper

2 dozen oysters

To make the mornay sauce, mix half of the Parmesan and mustard into the white sauce, then add the cream, season and mix (page 131).

Scrub the oysters and open (this is where the experienced hand comes in). Cut the oysters free from their shells and leave aside. Discard the shallow shells. Put a little mornay sauce into the deep shells, place the oyster on top, and cover with a little more of the sauce. Sprinkle with the remaining Parmesan. Place the oysters on a baking tray and brown under a hot grill for 3–4 minutes; alternatively, put into a hot oven (220°C/425°F/Gas 7) until brown. Serve with lemon wedges and brown bread.

Sister Anna takes a break from her duties, outside the Restaurant

Chaplain Dom Paul
McDonnell from Glenstal

George, Duc de Stacpoole, a long-time friend of Kylemore Abbey, gives us the following recollection:

'It is remembered here that when King Edward VII visited Connemara in 1907, he enjoyed the local oysters so much that he gave a special order for some to be sent to Buckingham Palace. The Dawros oyster beds belonged to the Mitchell Henry estate of Kylemore, and up to 1939 supplies were sent regularly to Cobh for the Cunard Liners.'

HONEYED TROUT

4 trout, medium size
1 tbsp honey
rind and juice of 1 lemon
1 tbsp chopped dill

freshly ground black pepper
lemon wedges and sprigs of dill to
  garnish

Gut the trout, remove the fins, and the heads if desired, wash and dry well.

Mix together all the other ingredients. Arrange the fish on a greased ovenproof dish, put a little of the dressing into the cavity, and brush the remainder over the fish. Cover the dish and bake for 20 minutes in a preheated fairly hot oven (200°C/400°F/Gas 6). Garnish with the sprigs of dill and lemon wedges.

POACHED HAKE WITH BUTTER SAUCE

4 x 170 g/6 oz fillets of hake
1.2 litres/2 pints/5 cups good fish
  stock
6 spring onions, finely chopped
175 ml/6 fl oz/¾ cup white wine
juice of ½ lemon

225 g/½ lb/1 cup butter
1 tbsp cream
salt and pepper
lemon wedges and fennel sprigs to
  garnish

Poach the hake very gently in the stock for 10–15 minutes. Remove from the saucepan on to a warm dish, and keep hot until the sauce is made.

Put the onions in a saucepan with the wine and bring to the boil. Continue boiling over a moderate heat until the mixture is reduced by half, then add the lemon juice. Cut the butter, which should come straight from the fridge, into little knobs. Add to the reduced liquid and whisk continuously over a gentle heat. Stir in the cream and seasoning. Do not allow to boil. Pour the sauce on to a serving dish and place the hake on top. Garnish with the fennel and lemon wedges.

HERRINGS IN OATMEAL WITH HORSERADISH SAUCE

4 herrings, gutted, with heads, tails
  and fins removed
75 g/3 oz/¾ cup oatmeal

45 g/1½ oz/3 tbsp butter
horseradish sauce (below)

Wash and dry the herrings. Coat with the oatmeal, pressing it well into the fish on both sides. Heat the butter in a frying pan and fry the herrings on both sides for 5–6 minutes, until golden brown. Drain on kitchen paper. Serve with the Horseradish Sauce.

Horseradish Sauce

225 ml/8 fl oz/1 cup cream
2 tbsp freshly grated horseradish
squeeze of lemon juice
l tsp caster sugar (US superfine
  sugar)

¼ tsp dry mustard
l tsp vinegar
pinch of pepper and salt

Gently whip the cream — it should not be stiff. Combine all the other ingredients and fold into the cream. Mix well and serve.

TIM'S ATLANTIC POLLOCK IN OATMEAL WITH GOOSEBERRY SAUCE

&

4 x 170 g/6 oz fillets of pollock
salt and pepper
55 g/2 oz/4 tbsp melted butter
75 g/3 oz/¾ cup coarse oatmeal

110 g/4 oz smoked bacon fat
lemon quarters
Gooseberry Sauce (below)

Season the fillets and dip in the melted butter. Coat the fillets with the oatmeal. Heat the bacon fat until sizzling and fry the fillets for 4 minutes on each side. Arrange on a hot dish and serve with the Gooseberry Sauce. Garnish with the lemon quarters.

This recipe comes from our good friend Tim O'Sullivan in Renvyle House.

Gooseberry Sauce

30 g/1 oz/2 tbsp butter
340 g/12 oz gooseberries, topped
   and tailed

½ tsp ground ginger
sugar to taste

Melt the butter in a saucepan and add the gooseberries. Cover with a lid and cook gently. When the fruit is soft (about 15 minutes) remove and liquidise until smooth. Return to the saucepan, add the ginger and sugar to taste, and serve.

MEAT AND POULTRY

✦

*T*he days when the Monastery provided its own meat from the flock of mountain sheep have long since gone. During those early times up to five or six sheep were butchered every week on the farm, with much scalding and scouring and sharpening of knives. Mountain sheep are leaner and smaller than valley sheep, and they yield a lot less meat. It is recalled that it would take six or seven chops to satisfy the average man's appetite. Every bit of the carcass was used, including the heart, liver and kidneys, and savoury puddings were made from the blood. Pork and beef were used infrequently, and were regarded as a great treat. Mutton was the usual fare, and many recipes for breaking the monotony of this meat were devised by the late, much loved Sister Bernadette, whose humility and simplicity endeared her to her Sisters. Sister Bernadette was that rarity, an instinctive natural cook.

The hatching of chickens, ducks and geese was very much part of the farmyard activity, and provided an alternative to mutton. Getting them ready for the table was a laborious task, since they had to be killed and then plucked by hand while still warm. The fractious pin feathers had to be extracted one by one. Then the carcass was hung for several days before being drawn; a minimum of twelve chickens were required for a single meal.

With today's efficient farming methods, lambs are brought on more quickly, and are killed at one year old. Today's lambs are raised in the valleys, and Connemara lamb is noted for its special sweet herb flavour derived from the limestone soil and local herbs. This lamb is the meat most frequently used today.

SAUTÉ OF CHICKEN WITH GARLIC AND WINE VINEGAR

꙳

1 medium chicken
1 tbsp vegetable oil
280 ml/½ pint/1¼ cups red wine vinegar

1 clove of garlic, peeled and crushed
2 tomatoes, peeled, deseeded and chopped

31

1 tbsp tomato purée
bouquet garni (parsley, thyme, bay
  leaf)

280 ml/½ pint/1¼ cups chicken
  stock
30 g/1 oz/2 tbsp butter
salt and freshly ground black
  pepper

Divide the chicken into 6 pieces and season. Heat the oil, add the chicken pieces and fry until lightly browned. Add the wine vinegar and the crushed garlic, cover and cook gently for 30 minutes. Add the tomatoes together with the purée and the bouquet garni. Continue to cook until the chicken is tender. Remove the chicken from the frying pan and put into a deep serving dish; keep warm. Add the chicken stock to the juices and boil to reduce. Strain the sauce into a saucepan, add a few knobs of butter and whisk, heat but do not boil. Season and pour over the chicken pieces. Serve with boiled rice, or mashed potatoes.

HERBED ROAST CHICKEN

1 x 900 g–1.4 kg/2–3 lb chicken
salt and freshly ground black
  pepper
1 tbsp chopped fresh thyme
1 tbsp chopped fresh tarragon
½ tbsp chopped fresh marjoram

½ tbsp chopped fresh parsley
110 g/4 oz/½ cup butter
juice of ½ lemon
1 clove of garlic, peeled and
  chopped
150 ml/¼ pint/⅔ cup chicken stock

Wash and dry the chicken and season well. Mix the herbs, butter, lemon juice and garlic in a bowl and season. Loosen the skin around the neck of the chicken and, as far as possible, the breast, without tearing the skin. Spread the herb butter under the skin and all over the top of the chicken. Place on a roasting pan. Cover the chicken in foil and roast in a preheated hot oven (220°C/425°F/Gas 7) for 50 minutes. Remove the foil, baste the chicken with the juices and brown in the oven for a further 10 minutes. Transfer to a serving dish, allow the juices in the roasting pan to settle, remove the fat, add the chicken stock, return the pan to the heat for a minute and pour the remaining juices over the chicken when serving. When carving, ensure that each serving has a little of both leg and breast. Serve with roast potatoes and seasonal vegetables.

CHICKEN AND PEPPER CASSEROLE

——————— ૨ૐ ———————

2 tbsp olive oil

1 chicken, jointed (US cut up)

175 ml/6 fl oz/¾ cup white wine

salt and freshly ground black pepper

1 tbsp chopped fresh marjoram and thyme

1 tbsp chopped fresh parsley

2 onions, peeled and chopped

2 cloves of garlic, peeled and crushed

2 red peppers, peeled, deseeded and sliced

1 green pepper, peeled, deseeded and sliced

4 tomatoes, skinned, deseeded and chopped

chopped parsley to garnish

Heat half the oil in a frying pan and brown the chicken pieces on both sides. Remove with a slotted spoon and put into a casserole dish. Add the wine, seasoning and chopped herbs. Cover and cook for 1 hour in a preheated moderate oven (180°C/350°F/Gas 4). Heat the remaining oil in the frying pan, add the onions and garlic and cook gently until soft, add the peppers and cook for 2–3 minutes. Finally, add the tomatoes and seasoning, cook for a further few minutes over a low heat. Halfway through cooking the chicken, add the peppers and onion mixture to the casserole dish. Cook until the chicken is tender, sprinkle with chopped parsley and serve with mashed potatoes or pasta.

SISTER CARMEL'S SHIN BEEF CASSEROLE

——————— ૨ૐ ———————

675 g/1½ lb shin beef, cut into small pieces

2 onions, peeled and sliced

2 carrots, scraped and sliced

1 stick of celery, washed and sliced

2 cloves of garlic, peeled and crushed

salt and freshly ground pepper

2 tbsp tomato purée

425 ml/¾ pint/1¾ cups water

1 tbsp cornflour to thicken

Put the meat into a casserole, add the vegetables and the garlic, and season. Blend the tomato purée with the water and pour over the meat and vegetables, cover and simmer on a very low heat for about 2 hours. When cooked, thicken with the cornflour blended with a little water, and boil for a minute before serving with plain boiled potatoes.

This recipe, which is a very old one, comes from the home of Kylemore's youngest postulant, Sister Carmel. Shin beef is very flavoursome and succulent, but we are advised that it is best not to fry it as one might do with other casseroles.

ROAST LEG OF SPRING LAMB WITH GARLIC AND THYME

1 x 2.2–2.8 kg/5–6 lb leg of spring lamb
5 cloves of garlic, peeled
10–12 small sprigs of thyme

55 g/2 oz/4 tbsp butter, melted
freshly ground black pepper and salt

Gravy

1 tbsp flour
pepper and salt

280 ml/½ pint/1¼ cups stock

Trim the leg and wipe over with a damp cloth. Split the garlic cloves in two. With a sharp knife make small incisions at intervals on the skin of the lamb, and insert a piece of garlic into each incision. Insert the sprigs of thyme in a similar manner. Brush over the leg with the butter, and season with black pepper and salt. Place on a roasting pan and cook in a preheated hot oven (220°C/420°F/Gas 7) for 20 minutes. Reduce the heat to (180°C/350°F/ Gas 4) and continue to cook for 15 minutes per 450 g/1 lb, basting occasionally. At this point the lamb is pink. Continue to cook for a further 20 minutes if well-done lamb is preferred. Remove from the pan, and allow to set before carving. Lamb is best carved fairly thickly.

To make the gravy, allow the sediment to set in the pan, then strain off the fat, being careful to leave all the sediment behind. Sprinkle the flour into the pan to absorb the sediment. Add the seasoning and mix well, cook over a low heat for a few minutes, then pour on the stock, bring to the boil, strain, and keep hot. Pour a little over the lamb when serving, and serve the remainder in a separate sauce-boat.

Sister Marie Bernard carrying feed for the cattle

IRISH STEW

———————— ❧ ————————

675 g/1½ lb boneless stewing lamb

900 g/2 lb medium-sized potatoes, peeled

2 carrots, scraped and sliced

2 good-sized onions, peeled and quartered

1 leek, washed and sliced

salt and pepper

575 ml/1 pint/2½ cups stock *or* water

1 tbsp chopped parsley

Trim the meat and cut into bite-sized pieces. Trim the potatoes to an even size. Put the meat, potato trimmings, carrots, onions and leek into a saucepan; season and pour on the stock. Bring to the boil and skim; continue to simmer for 1 hour. Place the potatoes on top; continue to simmer for a further 30 minutes. Remove the potatoes and keep warm. Check seasoning.

Put the stew into a heated deep serving dish. Place the potatoes on top, sprinkle with parsley and serve.

DEVILLED LAMB CUTLETS

———————— ❧ ————————

1 tbsp lemon juice

150 ml/¼ pint/⅔ cup cream

1 tbsp mango chutney — chop any large pieces finely

½ tbsp dry mustard

½ tbsp soya sauce

½ tbsp Worcester sauce

½ tbsp tomato purée

salt and freshly ground black pepper

8 centre-loin lamb cutlets

sprigs of parsley to garnish

Combine the lemon juice and the cream in a bowl. Add the chutney, mustard, soya sauce, Worcester sauce, tomato purée and seasoning. Mix well and brush the cutlets on one side with the mixture. Place the cutlets, brushed side up, under a preheated grill and cook for 8 minutes. Reduce the heat a little if necessary. Turn the cutlets, brush with the mixture, and grill until cooked. Any remaining mixture can be brushed on to the cutlets as they cook. Transfer to a warm serving dish and garnish with the sprigs of parsley.

SISTER BERNADETTE'S MUTTON AND PRUNE STEW

———————————— ❧ ————————————

675 g/1½ lb shank and lap of
  mutton
a little seasoned flour
a little dripping
1 onion, peeled and sliced

1 carrot, scraped and sliced
225 g/½ lb prunes (ready to use)
salt and pepper
water

Remove the skin and fat from the meat and cut into bite-sized pieces. Roll the meat in the seasoned flour, melt the dripping in a heavy casserole and fry the meat until brown. Remove from the casserole. Add the onion and cook gently until soft. Return the meat to the casserole, add the carrot and the prunes and pour on enough water to barely cover. Simmer gently for 2½–3 hours, season and skim. The gravy should be thick and brown.

FILLET OF PORK WITH HERB CHEESE STUFFING

———————————— ❧ ————————————

4 x 140 g/5 oz pork fillet pieces
  (US tenderloin)
1 tbsp chopped fresh parsley
1 tbsp chopped fresh thyme

1 tbsp chopped fresh oregano
110 g/4 oz cream cheese
salt and freshly ground black
  pepper

Slit the fillet pieces lengthwise but do not cut through, spread them out between two sheets of dampened greaseproof paper and flatten with a rolling pin. Chop the herbs and mix well in a bowl with the cream cheese; season with salt and freshly ground black pepper. Spread the cheese mixture down the centre of each fillet piece and roll up. Wrap them individually in foil and put into a roasting pan. Cook in a preheated moderate oven (180°C/350°F/Gas 4) for 20 minutes, remove the foil and slice each fillet into four pieces. Serve garnished with some of the fresh herbs.

STEWED RABBIT

———— ❧ ————

2 young rabbits, prepared and
  jointed (US cut up)
55 g/2 oz/4 tbsp margarine *or* 2
  tbsp vegetable oil
55 g/2 oz/½ cup seasoned flour
2 onions, peeled and sliced
110 g/4 oz bacon, cut into small
  pieces

55 g/2 oz/½ cup flour
1.5 litres/2½ pints/6 cups stock
1 stick of celery, chopped
2 carrots, scraped and sliced
salt and pepper
chopped parsley *or* chives

Wash the rabbit pieces well in cold salted water, and dry. Dip the rabbit
pieces in the seasoned flour, and shake off any excess. Melt the fat in a heavy
stew pan, add the rabbit pieces and fry quickly on both sides; remove and
keep hot. Add the onions and the bacon, sauté for 2–3 minutes, remove from
the casserole and add to the rabbit pieces. Add flour to the casserole and mix
well. Gently pour in the stock, bring to boiling point stirring all the time, add
the celery and the carrots. Return the rabbit and the bacon to the casserole,
check seasoning and simmer for 1½ hours. Put into a heated serving dish,
sprinkle with the parsley or chives, and serve with boiled potatoes.

ROAST DUCK WITH APPLE STUFFING

———— ❧ ————

1 oven-ready duck, 1.4–1.8 kg/3–4 lb

Wash and dry the duck. Prick the skin all over with a fork to allow the
excess fat to escape. Rub the skin with salt and season the cavity.

Apple Stuffing

4 scallions (US green onions),
  finely chopped
55 g/2 oz streaky bacon, diced
55 g/2 oz/4 tbsp butter, melted
2 large cooking apples, peeled,
  cored and chopped
1 tbsp lemon juice

140 g/5 oz/2½ cups white
  breadcrumbs
1 tbsp chopped parsley
salt and freshly ground black
  pepper
1 egg yolk

Sister Bernard with
visiting Sister Gonza

Cook the scallions and the bacon in the melted butter over a gentle heat until soft. Sprinkle the apples with the lemon juice, and add to the pan together with the breadcrumbs, herbs and seasoning. Mix and allow the stuffing to cool; bind with the egg yolk.

Put the stuffing into the cavity of the bird, truss, put on a roasting pan in a preheated moderate oven (180°C/350°F/Gas 4) for 1½ hours; baste occasionally during the cooking. Serve with apple sauce, roast potatoes and fresh garden peas.

Apple Sauce

2 good-sized cooking apples, peeled and sliced	sugar to sweeten
a little water	30 g/1 oz/2 tbsp butter

Put the apples into a saucepan with just enough water to keep them from sticking; cook gently until pulped. Blend to a smooth purée. Add a little sugar. Cut the butter into small pieces and stir into the puréed apples.

MICHAELMAS GOOSE WITH POTATO STUFFING

1 oven-ready goose, 4.5 kg/10 lb	30 g/1 oz/4 tbsp flour
salt	280 ml/½ pint/1¼ cups stock

Sage and Onion Stuffing

1 large onion finely chopped	¼ tsp dry mustard
55 g/2 oz/4 tbsp butter	1 egg yolk
1 tbsp chopped fresh sage	milk to moisten
225 g/8 oz/4 cups breadcrumbs	salt and pepper

Sweat the onion in the butter until soft. Mix all the other ingredients together, add the softened onion and mix well. Leave aside until ready to use.

Potato Stuffing

2 small onions, finely chopped
170 g/6 oz/¾ cup butter
1.150 kg/2½ lb mashed potatoes

4 tbsp chopped fresh parsley
2 tbsp chopped fresh thyme
salt and pepper

Cook the onions in 30 g/1 oz/2 tbsp butter until soft, melt the remaining butter and combine all the ingredients. Mix well, check seasoning, and leave aside until ready to use.

To prepare, stuff and roast goose

Wash the goose well inside and outside and dry thoroughly. Rub a little salt in the cavity, and on the skin. Stuff the neck with the sage and onion stuffing, fold the skin over to the back and secure with a skewer. Put the potato stuffing into the cavity and secure the body opening: the best way to do this is with a needle and thread. Prick the skin of the bird at intervals to allow fat to escape, put on a rack in a roasting pan and roast for 3 hours in a moderate oven (180°C/350°F/Gas 4). Cover the breast and drum sticks with foil or greaseproof paper if browning too quickly.

To make gravy, remove most of the fat from the roasting pan, sprinkle in a little flour and cook for 1 minute, add stock stirring all the time, boil, skim and season.

Serve the goose with gravy and apple sauce (page 40), add a dish of peas and you have a feast to remember.

STUFFED SHEEPS' HEARTS

─────────── ❧ ───────────

3 sheeps' hearts
a little fat to roast
30 g/1 oz/4 tbsp flour

150 ml/¼ pint/⅔ cup stock
salt and pepper

Stuffing

225 g/8 oz/4 cups fresh
  breadcrumbs
1 medium onion, finely chopped
salt and freshly ground black
  pepper

2 tbsp chopped fresh parsley
1 tbsp chopped fresh thyme
55 g/2 oz/4 tbsp margarine
1 egg, beaten

To make the stuffing

Mix all the dry ingredients together, rub in the margarine and bind with the egg.

Wash the hearts in cold salted water several times, cut out the blood vessels and slit into the hearts with a sharp knife making a good cavity. Wash again and dry well. Put the stuffing into the cavities and secure with a skewer. Heat the fat in an ovenproof dish and brush the hearts all over with the melted fat. Put the hearts into the oven dish, cover and cook in a moderate oven (180°C/350°F/Gas 4) for 1½ hours. Remove the hearts from the dish and keep warm. Allow the fat in the dish to settle and then drain off, leaving the sediment in the dish. Sprinkle in the flour and cook for 1 minute. Add the stock, bring to the boil, and allow to cook for 2–3 minutes. Season, skim and strain. Carve the hearts into thick slices, put on to a warm serving dish, and serve with the gravy.

This dish, as well as being very economical, is quite delicious. What a pity it has all but disappeared from today's home cooking!

KIDNEYS WITH MUSHROOMS AND ONIONS

8 lamb kidneys

30 g/1 oz/2 tbsp butter

2 medium onions, peeled and sliced

30 g/1 oz/4 tbsp flour

425 ml/¾ pint/1¾ cups stock

bouquet garni (parsley, thyme, bay leaf)

salt and freshly ground black pepper

170 g/6 oz mushrooms, sliced

1 tsp tomato purée

chopped parsley to garnish

Remove the fat from the kidneys, skin and cut each kidney in two, then remove the little piece of inner fat. Melt the butter in a frying pan and gently cook the onions until soft, add the kidneys and cook for 5–6 minutes, stirring all the time. Add the flour and mix, then pour in the stock, and slowly bring to the boil while stirring; add the bouquet garni, seasoning, mushrooms and tomato purée, and simmer for 1 hour or until the kidneys are tender. Remove the bouquet garni. Sprinkle with the parsley and serve with plain boiled rice.

BOILED OX TONGUE — HOT OR COLD

——————————— ❧ ———————————

1 ox tongue
1 onion, peeled and quartered
1 carrot, scraped and sliced

1 bay leaf and a few sprigs of parsley

Soak the ox tongue overnight in cold water. Put into a large saucepan with the other ingredients, cover with water, bring to the boil and simmer for about 3 hours. When the tongue is cooked, put it into a large bowl of cold water for a few minutes to cool, then remove the outer tough skin. Trim the root and remove the bones.

To serve hot, carve the tongue and serve either with parsley or mustard sauce, to which you have added a little of the cooking water.

To serve cold, put the tongue into a tin or bowl (it should fit tightly) and shape into a round, bringing the tip of the tongue towards the root. Pour over about a cup of the liquid in which the tongue was cooked, place a plate on top and a heavy weight over that, and leave until quite cold. Put into a fridge for a few hours, remove from the bowl and carve horizontally in very thin slices. Serve with sharp chutney or wholegrain mustard.

Mustard Sauce

To 280 ml/½ pint/1¼ cups white sauce (page 131) add 1 tsp made mustard and 1 tbsp vinegar.

Parsley Sauce

To 280 ml/½ pint/1¼ cups white sauce (page 131) add 1 tbsp finely chopped parsley.

BACON AND BEAN CASSEROLE

30 g/1 oz/2 tbsp butter

675 g/1½ lb collar bacon, cut into cubes

1 onion, peeled and sliced

1 leek, washed and sliced

2 sticks of celery, washed and finely chopped

1 carrot, scraped and diced

30 g/1 oz/4 tbsp flour

2 tbsp tomato purée

280 ml/½ pint/1¼ cups chicken stock

280 ml/½ pint/1¼ cups cider

225 g/8 oz/1¼ cups haricot beans, soaked and cooked

2 cloves of garlic, crushed

1 tbsp sage and marjoram mixed

salt and freshly ground black pepper

Melt the butter in a casserole dish. Add the bacon, and cook lightly for 3 minutes. Add the onion, leek, celery and carrot, and continue to cook for a further 5 minutes. Add the flour and tomato purée, and mix well. Pour on the chicken stock and cider, and bring to the boil, stirring continuously. Lower the heat and add the haricot beans, garlic and herbs; season to taste. Place a lid on the dish and cook in a preheated oven (170°C/325°F/Gas 3) for 2 hours. Serve with floury potatoes.

CHRISTMAS

The Feast of Christmas

*I*n this Monastery, Christmas begins on 21 December. An old Belgian custom was brought by the Community to Ireland, and to this day, on the evening of 20 December, the Nuns file out of Choir (Chapel) and assemble in silence outside the Community room door. The Abbess passes in, lights the Christmas candle in the darkened room and kneels to pray, silently, in thanksgiving for all the year has brought and to ask the Lord's mercy on herself and her Sisters. Then, the strains of a harp fill the air and the voices of the Nuns waft heavenward with the ancient antiphon:

> 'Nolite timere! Nolite timere! Quinta enim, enim die;
> Nolite timere! Nolite timere! Quinta enim, enim die
> Nolite timere! Veniet Dominus Noster!'

> *'Fear not! Fear not! In five days, five days*
> *Fear not! Fear not! In five, only five days*
> *Our Lord will come!'*

Then follows the beautiful versicle, sung with feeling by the Chantress:

> 'Rorate coeli desuper, et nubes pluant justum!'
> *'Let the heavens part and the clouds rain down justice!'*

The choir responds:

> 'Aperiatur terra et germinet salvatorem!'
> *'Let the earth open and bud forth salvation!'*

The great 'O' antiphon of that evening at Vespers is 'O clavis David' (O key of David . . . the key which opens and no one closes). The reference is to the Christ Jesus, Whose coming into our world opens the gates of paradise, removing the darkness of sin and evil, and freeing us, His people, to enter peace and joy.

Then the Nuns enter the room and wish one another 'Happy Christmas'.

Christmas Supper follows: traditional turkey and ham served with cranberrry sauce. There are merry faces; the novices and postulants try to come to terms with the anticipation of the feast, and wonder; tomorrow we shall be back to the Advent liturgy and still waiting in 'joyful hope for the coming of Our Lord Jesus Christ'.

Mother Clare Morley O.S.B.

Christmas Day

*C*hristmas Eve comes to a close in the Choir (Chapel) with vigils and Midnight Mass. The lights are lit on the tree and the Nuns share tea and Christmas cake with friends and visitors who come to celebrate the birth of Christ with us.

Then it is off to bed in anticipation of one of the few luxuries we Nuns allow ourselves in the year — a lie-in on Christmas morning! Morning Lauds and Conventual Mass are moved from 6 a.m. to 8.30 a.m. on this special day.

After Mass, all have breakfast together; all meals are shared every day, but Christmas Day has always been special. The refectory is filled with Christmas decorations and gifts. Each person receives a small token gift from the Abbess.

After breakfast, the Nuns gather around the life-size Crib to sing carols. Then it is time to prepare for the Christmas Dinner. The house is unusually quiet: the students have all gone home and the staff are with their families. It is a rare luxury to be free from the labours of our everyday work, to share this time without care.

The recipes for this traditional meal are a link with those who have gone before us: the stuffing for the turkey; the chutney with the ham; brandy butter for the pud — all accompanied by a glass of wine to enhance the flavour!

The Nuns come together in the Choir for evening prayer, Vespers, giving thanks not just for a lovely day, but more importantly for the birth of Christ: 'Verbum caro factum est', 'The Word was made flesh'. Isn't this what Christmas is all about?

Sister Magdalena FitzGibbon O.S.B.

Christmas Dinner

Light Carrot and Orange Soup

Roast Stuffed Turkey and Gravy
Patricia's Cranberry Sauce
Glazed Ham
Braised Red Cabbage
Celery au Gratin

Christmas Pudding
Ypres Wine Cream
Old-fashioned Sherry Trifle

LIGHT CARROT AND ORANGE SOUP

55 g/2 oz/4 tbsp butter

2 medium onions, peeled and sliced

450 g/1 lb carrots, scraped and roughly diced

1 stick of celery, washed and chopped with coarse strings removed

30 g/1 oz/4 tbsp flour

1.2 litres/2 pints/5 cups good chicken stock

2 tomatoes, quartered

salt and freshly ground black pepper

juice of 2 oranges

chopped chives to garnish

Heat the butter in a saucepan and slowly sweat the onions until soft, add the carrots and celery and continue to cook for 2–3 minutes. Sprinkle in the flour and mix well. Pour on the stock, add the tomatoes, bring to the boil and simmer for 1 hour. Blend in a food processor until smooth. Return to the saucepan to heat. Season, add the orange juice and serve garnished with chives.

ROAST STUFFED TURKEY AND GRAVY

———————— ❧ ————————

1 x 5.5 kg/12 lb free-range hen
 turkey

55 g/2 oz/4 tbsp butter

salt and pepper

Gravy

425–575 ml/¾–1 pint/1¾–2½ cups
 stock — preferably giblet *or*
 turkey

a little flour

salt and pepper

Stuffing

75 g/3 oz/6 tbsp butter

1 onion, peeled and finely chopped

450 g/1 lb/8 cups fresh white
 breadcrumbs

2 tbsp chopped parsley

1 tbsp chopped thyme

salt and pepper

55 g/2 oz/⅓ cup finely diced ham

1 egg, beaten

a little turkey stock

First make the stuffing, preferably the night before.

Melt the butter and use just a little of it to sweat the onion until it is soft. Put the breadcrumbs, herbs, seasoning and ham into a bowl and mix. Add the remaining melted butter, the egg, a little stock, and bind all together.

Any of the following additions are very good with bread stuffing:

minced celery and carrots

chopped apricots and raisins

sausagemeat

Wash the turkey well inside and outside, thoroughly dry, and just before cooking put the stuffing into the crop of the bird and any remaining stuffing into the body. Fasten back the neck skin with a skewer and stitch the body opening. Tie the drumsticks to the tail of the bird and fold back the wings. Butter the breast and legs. Place the bird on a large sheet of foil and wrap as if you are making a parcel. Place on a roasting pan into a preheated oven (180°C/350°F/Gas 4) for 4 hours. Test with a skewer to ensure the juices run clear. Half an hour before the bird is cooked, remove the foil, baste well and allow to brown.

To make the gravy, strain off most of the fat from the pan making sure to retain the sediment. Put sufficient flour in the pan to blend with the juices, add the stock and boil for a few minutes. Season, strain and serve.

PATRICIA'S CRANBERRY SAUCE

450 g/1 lb cranberries
55 g/2 oz/4 tbsp sugar
3 tbsp water

juice and rind of 1 orang
90 ml/3 fl oz/⅓ cup brandy

Put the cranberries, sugar, water, juice and rind of orange into a saucepan and simmer gently until soft, but not overcooked. Add the brandy, allow to cool and serve.

GLAZED HAM

4.5–5.5 kg/10–12 lb ham
1 carrot
1 onion
a few peppercorns
bay leaf

75 g/3 oz/¾ cup brown sugar
2 tbsp made mustard (US
   prepared mustard)
cloves
175 ml/6 fl oz/¾ cup cider

Wash the ham well, scrape, and soak in cold water overnight. Place the ham in a large saucepan and cover with cold water to which you have added the carrot, onion, peppercorns and bay leaf. Bring the ham to the boil and simmer for 2½–3 hours or until it is nearly cooked. Remove the ham from the saucepan and peel off skin. Mix the sugar and mustard together. Stud the ham with cloves, coat with the mustard mixture, and put it into a roasting pan. Pour in the cider and bake for a further 1 hour in a warm oven (170°C/325°F/Gas 3), or until the ham is fully cooked and nicely browned all over. Baste the ham occasionally during the cooking, remove from the pan and serve on a large meat dish.

CHRISTMAS RED CABBAGE

½ tbsp oil

30 g/1 oz/2 tbsp butter

1 red onion, peeled, quartered and sliced

¼ head red cabbage

110 g/4 oz redcurrant jelly

1 eating apple, quartered and thinly sliced

salt and freshly ground black pepper

In a heavy-bottomed pan, heat the oil and butter. Add the onion and cook gently for 1 minute. Add the shredded red cabbage and cook for 10 minutes. In another pot, melt the redcurrant jelly, add the apple and cook for 1 minute; then add the redcurrant mixture to the cabbage, mix well, season and serve immediately.

CELERY AU GRATIN

1 head of celery, trimmed, scrubbed and cut into 5 cm/2 inch pieces

75 g/3 oz Cheddar cheese, grated

½ tsp made mustard (US prepared mustard)

425 ml/¾ pint/1¾ cups white sauce (page 131)

salt and cayenne pepper

2 tbsp breadcrumbs

Cook the celery in boiling salted water (add a little turkey stock to the water if you have it). Drain and keep warm. Add half the cheese and the mustard to the white sauce; season. Put alternate layers of the sauce and the celery into an ovenproof dish, ending with the sauce. Mix the remaining cheese with the breadcrumbs and sprinkle on top. Put under a preheated grill to brown.

The magnificent fireplace in the Drawing-room

Cooking the Christmas Dinner. From the left: Sister Dorothy, Sister Peter, Sister Bernard, Sister Magdalena and Mother Clare

CHRISTMAS PUDDING

—————————— 🐚 ——————————

450 g/1 lb/2⅔ cups seedless raisins

450 g/1 lb/2⅔ cups golden sultanas (US golden raisins)

225 g/½ lb/1⅓ cups muscatel raisins (US white raisins)

225 g/½ lb/1⅓ cups currants

110 g/4 oz/1 cup mixed peel (US candied citrus peel)

110 g/4 oz/½ cup glacé cherries (US candied cherries)

450 g/1 lb/2 cups brown sugar

450 g/1 lb/8 cups breadcrumbs

1 tsp mixed spice

½ tsp nutmeg

170 g/6 oz/1½ cups self-raising flour

450 g/1 lb/2 cups butter

2 tbsp honey

6 eggs, beaten

grated rind and juice of 1 lemon and 1 orange

175 ml/6 fl oz/¾ cup whiskey

280 ml/½ pint/1¼ cups bottle stout — you may need a little more

This quantity will make three two-pound puddings approximately, and it is best made at least 2 months before Christmas.

Mix all the dry ingredients very well together. Melt the butter, add to the honey, eggs, lemon rind and juice, whiskey and the stout. Stir well and add to the dry ingredients. The mixture should be quite moist; add a little extra stout if necessary. Leave to stand overnight, and next day fill pudding bowls to within about 3.8 cm/1½ inches from the rim. Cover with 2 layers of greaseproof paper (US parchment paper) and tie down the sides. Steam for 6 hours. Steam for a further 1–1½ hours on Christmas Day.

The Nuns have many Christmas pudding recipes. The one chosen here is from the home of Sister Magdalena and was made by her late mother over many years.

YPRES WINE CREAM (FOR CHRISTMAS PUDDING)

—————————— 🐚 ——————————

475 ml/16 fl oz/2 cups white wine

4 eggs

4 tsp sugar

2 tsp cornflour (US cornstarch)

Beat all the ingredients together in a saucepan and cook over a very low heat until it thickens, beating all the time.

This sauce is like an egg custard made with wine instead of milk. Its origin goes back to Ypres. It was never written down, just passed on by word of mouth from one kitchen Sister to the next. It is now recorded by Sister Benedict for the first time.

OLD-FASHIONED SHERRY TRIFLE

ঽ▲

1 home-made sponge cake
(page 96)

3 tbsp raspberry jam, preferably
home-made

110 ml/4 fl oz/½ cup sherry

575 ml/1 pint/2½ cups egg custard

425 ml/¾ pint/1¾ cups cream

a few glacé cherries (US candied
cherries) and chopped nuts to
decorate

Egg Custard

4 eggs

30 g/1 oz/2 tbsp sugar

575 ml/1 pint/2½ cups milk

First make the custard. Beat the eggs and the sugar, heat the milk and add to the eggs. Put into a saucepan, stir and heat very gently until the custard thickens a little and coats the back of the spoon. Do not allow to boil. Alternatively, you can make the custard in a double-boiler.

Split the sponge cake and sandwich halves together with the jam, cut into slices and then into fingers, about 3.8 cm/1½ inches wide. Place half the sponge cake in the bottom of a glass bowl and moisten with half the sherry, then continue with the remaining half of the sponge and the remaining sherry. When the custard is almost cold, pour over the sponge. Whip the cream and sweeten with the sugar. Pipe the cream over the custard and decorate with chopped nuts and halved cherries.

Leave the trifle to rest for several hours before using, allowing the sponge to soak up the sherry.

MINCE PIES

ঽ▲

Shortcrust Pastry

340 g/12 oz/3 cups flour

225 g/8 oz/1 cup butter

55 g/2 oz/½ cup icing sugar (US
powdered sugar)

1 egg yolk

pinch of salt

a little water

a little beaten egg

Make the pastry as instructed on page 101.

Mincemeat — Light and Fruity

55 g/2 oz/⅓ cup currants

55 g/2 oz/⅓ cup sultanas (US golden raisins)

55 g/2 oz/⅓ cup raisins

30 g/1 oz/¼ cup mixed peel (US candied citrus peel)

30 g/1 oz/¼ cup chopped almonds

grated rind and juice of 1 lemon

1 cooking apple, peeled and finely chopped

30 g/1 oz/2 tbsp dark brown sugar

¼ tsp nutmeg

30 g/1 oz/2 tbsp butter

30 g/1 oz crystallised ginger, chopped

1 banana, peeled and sliced

2 tbsp brandy

Mix all the ingredients together in a large bowl and allow to stand overnight before storing. Put into sterilised jars. This mincemeat should be used within four weeks of making.

Grease 12 patty tins. Roll out the pastry and cut into 12 rounds, using a 7.6 cm/3 inch fluted cutter, and another 12 rounds using a slightly smaller cutter. Line the tins with the larger rounds. Put a spoonful of mincemeat into each pie, dampen the edges, and place smaller rounds over the pies, firmly positioning the edges. With a knife, put a small slit on top of each pie, brush over with beaten egg and bake in a preheated hot oven (200°C/400°F/Gas 6) for 15–20 minutes.

To make larger quantities, adjust the recipe accordingly. As mince pies keep well, it is probably best to cook bigger quantities.

MULLED WINE

1 bottle red wine

40 ml/1½ fl oz/2½ tbsp brandy

juice of 1 freshly squeezed orange

1 level tbsp brown sugar (more if you like it sweet)

2 sticks of cinnamon

¼ tsp freshly grated nutmeg

½ lemon, sliced and studded with cloves

½ orange, sliced and studded with cloves

Pour the wine, brandy and orange juice into a saucepan. Add the sugar,

The stained-glass window in the Gothic Church

cinnamon and nutmeg. Place on a low heat and very slowly bring to simmering point. The flavours must be given time to absorb. Remove the cinnamon sticks and check sweetness. Add the fruit slices and serve in heated glasses, making sure there is a little fruit in each glass.

For a lighter punch, 280 ml/½ pint/1¼ cups water may be added to the wine, and this may need a little more sugar.

SISTER BENEDICT'S CHRISTMAS CAKE

340 g/12 oz/1½ cups butter
340 g/12 oz/1½ cups brown sugar
2 tbsp golden syrup
grated rind of 1 lemon
450 g/1 lb/4 cups flour
6 large eggs
1.4 kg/3 lb/8 cups mixed dried fruit
  (US light and dark raisins,
  currants)

110 g/4 oz/1 cup ground almonds
110 g/4 oz/1 cup chopped almonds,
  do not blanch
110 g/4 oz/½ cup glacé cherries
  (US candied cherries)
110 g/4 oz/1 cup chopped peel (US
  mixed candied citrus peel)
1 tsp mixed spice
1 tsp nutmeg
1 apple, grated

Cream the butter, sugar, golden syrup and lemon rind in a large bowl until light and fluffy. Sieve the flour and lightly beat the eggs. Combine all the other ingredients in a large bowl and mix well. Add the eggs gradually to the creamed butter and sugar, beating well between each addition. Do not allow to curdle, and if this happens add a little flour. Gently fold in the flour and finally mix in the fruit. Put the mixture into a 25 cm/10 inch cake tin/pan double-lined with greased greaseproof paper (US parchment paper), and bake in a cool oven (150°C/300°F/Gas 2) for approximately 4 hours. Test with a skewer to ensure the cake is cooked, remove from the oven and allow to cool in the tin/pan. Wrap in two layers of greaseproof paper, and store in an airtight tin until ready to ice.

Almond Paste

225 g/½ lb/1⅔ cups icing sugar
  (US powdered sugar)
225 g/½ lb/1 cup caster sugar (US
  superfine sugar)
450 g/1 lb/4 cups ground almonds

2 eggs
¼ tsp almond essence
2 tbsp whiskey
1 egg white, lightly beaten

Sieve the sugars and mix with the almonds. Beat the eggs, almond essence and whiskey together. Add to the sugar and almonds and mix to a stiff paste. Turn on to a board dusted with icing sugar and knead. Adjust this quantity for smaller or larger cakes.

To apply the almond paste: Roll out the paste to a little larger than the cake. Brush the top of the cake with lightly beaten egg white. Place the cake upside-down on to the paste. Brush the sides with egg white; spread the paste down the sides using a knife, keeping the edge sharp with the board. Turn over and store until applying the royal icing.

Royal Icing

900 g/2 lb/6⅔ cups icing sugar (US powdered sugar)
½ tsp glycerine

4 egg whites
1 tsp lemon juice

Sieve the icing sugar twice to ensure that it is completely free of any lumps. Put the egg whites into a large bowl and beat very slightly. Gradually add the icing sugar, beating well. Add the lemon juice and continue to beat until the icing stands in peaks. Add the glycerine. Cover with a damp cloth until ready to use. Adjust the quantity to suit the size of the cake.

To apply the royal icing: Place the cake on to an upturned plate. Spread the icing evenly over the top and sides of the cake, using a palette knife. Spike the icing all over, giving a snow effect. Allow it to dry thoroughly before storing.

St Stephen's Day

After that, things become more frugal.

GIBLET BROTH

turkey giblets (liver, gizzard, heart — also the neck)
1.7 litres/3 pints/7½ cups chicken *or* turkey stock
1 onion, peeled and diced

1 carrot, peeled and diced
1 stick of celery, washed and finely chopped
1 slice of turnip, peeled and diced
1 tbsp chopped parsley and thyme

<table>
<tr><td>1 bay leaf</td><td>55 g/2 oz/4 tbsp turkey fat</td></tr>
<tr><td>salt and freshly ground black
  pepper</td><td>55 ml/2 fl oz/¼ cup sherry</td></tr>
</table>

Wash the giblets in cold salted water, put into a large saucepan and cover with the stock. Bring to the boil and simmer for 1½ hours. Strain the liquid. Return it to a clear pan and add the vegetables, herbs and seasoning. Simmer for 20 minutes, add the sherry and serve.

Meat cut from the neck along with the trimmed and chopped giblets can be returned to the soup or reserved for using in stuffing.

TURKEY LEFTOVERS

——————————— ❧ ———————————

2 tbsp vegetable oil	55 g/2 oz/½ cup flour
1 leek, washed and sliced	850 ml/1½ pints/3¾ cups chicken
1 onion, peeled and finely chopped	*or* turkey stock
4 sticks of celery, washed and	450 g/1 lb cooked turkey meat,
chopped	skinned and cut in small pieces
1 pepper, deseeded and diced	150 ml/¼ pint/⅔ cup cream
1 carrot, scraped and diced	seasoning

Heat the oil in a saucepan and sauté the leek and onion until soft. Add all the other vegetables and fry for a few minutes. Mix in the flour and continue to cook for a further minute. Pour in the stock and gently bring to the boil, while continuing to stir. Simmer for 10 minutes but do not allow the vegetables to overcook. Add the turkey and reheat for 5 minutes. Remove from the heat, pour in the cream and check seasoning. Serve with plain boiled rice.

This recipe is delicious made into a pie using puff pastry.

EASTER

✣

Easter at Kylemore

The most solemn week of the liturgical year is that of Holy Week. Holy Thursday sees the beginning of the Sacred Triduum. These three days — Holy Thursday, Good Friday and Holy Saturday — are days of silence and recollection.

On Holy Thursday, twelve apostles are drawn from the friends and staff of the Community, to participate in the Mandatum, the symbolic ceremony of the washing of the feet. After Mass, supper is shared in silence with appropriate sacred music. On this evening, the Abbess serves supper to the Nuns.

After Good Friday's ceremonies, the Nuns partak:e of a penitential supper of prunes and brown bread which they eat on their knees.

The Mass of the Easter Vigil begins with the lighting of the paschal fire and the procession to the Chapel. This celebration of Mass is a very joyous one, with the resounding of bells once more. After the ceremonies, the Nuns, their friends and visitors join together for tea and Simnel cake.

Easter is a time of bells and light in monasteries. Appropriately, in Kylemore the Abbey slopes are usually ablaze with daffodils. It seems as if the daffodil bells are standing waiting to ring their Easter joy — Alleluia!

Easter Sunday is again a day for rejoicing and of true Community spirit, in the tradition started by St Benedict so many centuries ago: 'Surrexit Dominus verre', 'The Lord is truly risen'.

Sister Magdalena FitzGibbon O.S.B.

Easter Sunday Lunch

Chilled Melon and Orange Cups

Easter Lamb with Rosemary
Thin Gravy — Mint Sauce
Julienne of Carrot and Courgette
Plain Boiled Potatoes

Rhubarb Tart and Custard

CHILLED MELON AND ORANGE CUPS

1 galia *or* ogen melon
2 oranges, segmented (page 131)
2 tbsp lemon juice

1 tsp caster sugar (US superfine sugar)
1 tbsp Cointreau (US Orange Curaçao *or* Triple Sec)
mint leaves to garnish

Cut the melon in half and remove the seeds. Using a melon baller, remove the flesh and put into a large bowl. Scoop out any remaining flesh; avoid taking any of the hard flesh near the skin; chop small and add to bowl. Peel the oranges and segment them over a bowl to catch the juice. Add the oranges to the melon. Combine the lemon juice, caster sugar and Cointreau with the orange juice, pour over the fruit, mix, and cover the bowl with cling film. Refrigerate for a few hours. To serve, spoon into individual glasses and top with a sprig of mint.

EASTER LAMB WITH ROSEMARY

2.2–2.8 kg/5–6 lb leg of lamb, boned
salt and pepper
1 tbsp chopped rosemary
2 tbsp olive oil

3 cloves of garlic, peeled
1 tbsp flour
425 ml/¾ pint/1¾ cups stock
salt and freshly ground black pepper

Season the leg of lamb inside and out. Combine the rosemary with the olive oil. Rub the inside of the leg liberally with the rosemary and oil mixture, reserving some for the outside. Roll up the leg and tie. Brush the outside with the remaining oil and rosemary. With a sharp knife make three incisions in the leg and insert the whole cloves of garlic. Transfer the leg to a roasting pan and put into a preheated hot oven (220°C/425°F/Gas 7) for 10 minutes. Reduce heat to a moderate oven (180°C/ 350°F/Gas 4) and roast for 1½–2 hours, remembering to baste frequently. Remove the meat from the pan and keep warm. Drain the fat from the pan and sprinkle a little flour on to the sediment; mix well and cook for 1 minute. Add the stock, bring to the boil and simmer for a further minute or two. Skim, season and serve with the lamb.

RHUBARB TART AND CUSTARD

Using the recipe for Gooseberry Tart (page 105), replace the gooseberries with 675 g/1½ lb young rhubarb sliced into 2.5 cm/1 inch pieces.

Make the custard as instructed on page 53.

It is traditional in Kylemore Abbey to have the first rhubarb of the season on Easter Sunday.

SIMNEL CAKE

225 g/8 oz/1 cup butter

225 g/8 oz/1¼ cups caster sugar (US superfine sugar)

4 eggs

340 g/12 oz/3 cups flour

½ tsp ground ginger

½ tsp mixed spice (US cinnamon, clove, nutmeg)

1 tsp baking powder

280 g/10 oz/1⅔ cups sultanas (US golden raisins)

170 g/6 oz/1 cup currants

170 g/6 oz/1 cup raisins

75 g/3 oz/⅓ cup glacé cherries, halved (US candied cherries)

75 g/3 oz/¾ cup mixed peel (US candied citrus peel)

grated rind of 1 lemon and 1 orange

450 g/1 lb almond paste (pages 56–7)

1 egg, beaten

Line a 20 cm/8 inch cake tin/pan with two layers of greaseproof (US parchment) paper. Cream the butter and the sugar, beat the eggs lightly and add to the creamed mixture a little at a time, beating well after each addition. Sieve the flour and add the spices, salt and baking powder. Mix all the fruits together, add the grated lemon rind and juice and mix thoroughly. Fold the flour into the cake mixture. Stir in the fruits. Put half of the mixture into the cake tin, and smooth over. Roll out one-third of the almond paste to almost the size of the tin — about 19 cm/7½ inch diameter — and place on top of the cake mixture. Put the remainder of the cake mixture into the tin, smooth over the top and brush with a little cold water. Bake in a warm oven (160°C/325°F/ Gas 3) for 3½ hours. Test with a skewer before removing to ensure it is cooked. Cool the cake in the tin.

Cover the top of the cake with the remaining almond paste, and decorate with a criss-cross pattern, or, if you like, reserve a small piece of the almond paste to make little eggs or an Easter chicken. Brush the top of the cake with the beaten egg, and put in a hot oven (210°C/425°F/Gas 7) for a few minutes until slightly brown.

EASTER BISCUITS

110 g/4 oz/½ cup butter
110 g/4 oz/½ cup caster sugar (US superfine sugar)
1 egg, separated

200 g/7 oz/1¾ cups flour
pinch of salt
½ tsp ground cinnamon
55 g/2 oz/⅓ cup currants

Cream the butter and the sugar until light, and beat in the egg yolk. Sieve the flour, salt and cinnamon, and fold into the creamed mixture. Add the currants and mix. Turn on to a floured board and knead. Return to the bowl and leave in a fridge for 30 minutes before rolling out. Roll out thinly to less than 0.6 cm/¼ inch and cut into rounds about 5 cm/2 inches in diameter. Bake in a fairly hot oven (200°C/400°F/ Gas 6) for 10 minutes. Remove from the oven, brush over with the beaten egg white and sprinkle with a little caster sugar. Return to the oven for a further 5–8 minutes until the egg white is golden. Cool on a wire tray.

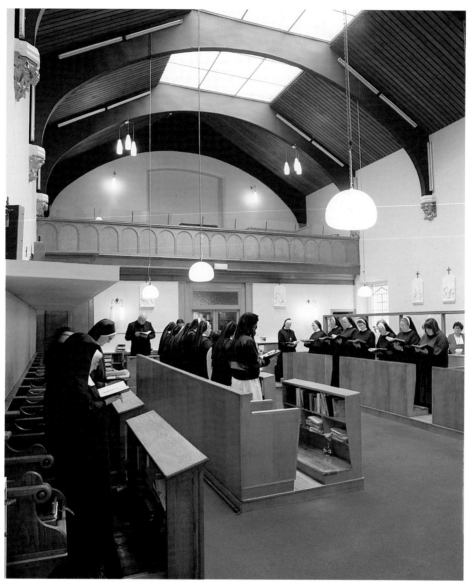

The Community at prayer in the Abbey Chapel

CHOCOLATE FUDGE WITH HAZELNUTS

575 ml/1 pint/2½ cups milk
900 g/2 lb/4 cups sugar
55 g/2 oz/½ cup cocoa

55 g/2 oz/4 tbsp butter
½ tsp vanilla essence
110 g/4 oz/1 cup chopped hazelnuts

Heat the milk with the sugar in a heavy saucepan, stirring until the sugar is dissolved. Add the cocoa, butter and vanilla essence, and bring to the boil, stirring continuously until the mixture is smooth. Boil until 116°C/240°F is reached on a sugar thermometer (soft ball stage); remove from the heat. Add the hazelnuts and continue to stir until the mixture is really stiff. Pour into a greased tin and leave until nearly cold, mark into squares, and when the fudge is set, cut through with a sharp knife. Store in an airtight container.

Fast and Festival

*T*he three great world religions have all had an influence on the food we eat, or, for that matter, do not eat. Judaism, Christianity and Islam have their laws in what may or what may not be eaten. The great Jewish feast of Passover lays down in detail the food to be eaten at the Seder meal. This meal was symbolic of the Israelites' slavery and the exodus from Egypt. Their sojourn in the desert involved the banning of food and meat which was unsuitable to the climate. Islam in turn had similar laws, and while Christianity did not ban foods, it prohibited the use of food and meats at special times of the year.

The main Christian period of fast was during Lent, but a lesser fast prevailed during Advent, on Ember Days, and the vigil of Christmas, the Assumption and All Saints (All Hallows, Hallowe'en). The old Lenten fast was extremely severe, and meat and dairy produce were forbidden. This explains the rush to use up dairy items on Shrove Tuesday (the day before the Lenten fast began on Ash Wednesday). We still make pancakes on Shrove Tuesday! Salted fish was much in demand, and when on Easter Sunday the monastic Brother Kitchener could serve a roast goose, he did so with salted herring as a jockey on top. There was one break in the Lenten severity, on Mothering Sunday, when serving girls were allowed to bake a Simnel cake to bring home when visiting their mothers.

The use of Easter lamb comes from the Christian liturgy as well as from the Jewish paschal meal. And after Lent a feast of eggs ensued, now remembered with chocolate eggs.

The other great Christian festival is that of Christmas and because it was in mid-winter the food was substantial, including rich puddings, cakes and game birds. The turkey was brought by conquistadors from the New World in the sixteenth century, and soon became the preferred Christmas dish, as it did for the American festival of Thanksgiving.

Some monastic customs are still retained, for example the blessing of wine on the feast of St John (27 December). The wine is blessed during Mass and distributed in the Refectory with a card saying, 'Caritas Sancti Joannis' (love of St John). Likewise bread is blessed on the feast of St Agatha (5 February).

Both the Church and monastic fasts have been greatly mitigated today. People are very conscious of diet and in many cases are more severe with themselves than the Church ever demanded.

The patron saints of cooks are St Lawrence and St Martha: the latter is an obvious one. St Lawrence was said to have been tortured to death on a gridiron; a twisted sense of Christian humour makes him the patron of those who work in hot kitchens.

Dom Paul McDonnell

Eggs, Milk and Cheese

❖

Sister Benedict who looks after the farm and the garden is convinced of the benefits to health of eating plenty of fresh produce — a point of view she passionately defends. This is what she has to say of dairy products:

'What a wonderful combination and what naturally healthy foods! So many satisfying dishes can be made using eggs, butter, cheese and milk, in a thousand and one variations. Add potatoes and a few vegetables and what more could one want? Until the Famine and the advent of imported foods, the Irish were the healthiest race in Europe, so take the advice of a leading heart surgeon in Ireland — eat sensibly and eat natural foods — your body was not designed to cope with artificial substitutes.'

An ever-increasing number of people would agree with her.

KEITH'S CHEESE AND MUSHROOM MOULDS

❧

1 onion, peeled and finely chopped
1 clove of garlic, peeled and crushed
65 g/2½ oz/5 tbsp butter
225 g/8 oz mushrooms, wiped and sliced
30 g/1 oz/4 tbsp flour

280 ml/½ pint/1¼ cups milk
55 g/2 oz/½ cup Cheddar cheese, grated
1 tbsp cream
salt and freshly ground black pepper
chopped parsley to garnish

Fry the onion and the garlic in 45 g/1½ oz/3 tbsp of the butter without colouring, add the mushrooms and cook for a few minutes until tender. Divide this mixture into four individual ovenproof dishes. Melt the remaining butter in a saucepan, add the flour and cook for a minute, then pour in the milk and, stirring continuously, bring to the boil. Cook gently until the sauce thickens. Mix half the cheese with the cream and add to the sauce; season. Pour the sauce over the mushroom and onion mixture and sprinkle with the remaining cheese. Bake for 12 minutes in a preheated moderate oven (180°C/350°F/Gas 4), and sprinkle with the chopped parsley before serving.

PRAWN AND MUSHROOM PANCAKES

30 g/1 oz/2 tbsp butter

170 g/6 oz frozen prawns

75 g/3 oz mushrooms

30 g/1 oz/4 tbsp flour

425 ml/¾ pint/1¾ cups cream

salt and freshly ground black
  pepper

75 g/3 oz/¾ cup grated white
  Cheddar cheese

Melt the butter in a pan, add the prawns and mushrooms, and heat gently: do not boil. Add the flour, mix, and pour in the cream slowly. Stir until thickened, season, and keep hot.

Divide the mixture between the pancakes. Roll up each pancake carefully and arrange them on a serving dish. Pour the remaining cream over the pancakes, sprinkle with grated cheese and brown under the grill.

Pancake Mix

2 eggs

225 g/8 oz/2 cups flour

575 ml/1 pint/2½ cups milk

pinch of salt

Beat the eggs lightly. Stir in the flour and enough milk to make a smooth paste. Gradually, add the rest of the milk. Beat until smooth and then leave to rest for 1 hour.

To make the pancakes: Put a lightly greased frying pan on high heat. When it is smoking, put in half a cup of batter for the first pancake. Cook until golden brown, turn, and cook on the other side. Continue this way, using up all the batter. Stack the pancakes on a plate, with greaseproof paper (US parchment paper) between each one, and keep in a warm oven.

SISTER BENEDICT'S CRÈME BOULLE

&

(HOME-MADE CREAM CHEESE)

Allow a quantity of unpasteurised milk to sour until it is quite solid, then let it drip through a muslin bag for 36 hours. The whey can be used for bread-making. Beat the curd until thick and creamy.

Use as a savoury dish by seasoning and adding herbs of choice, e.g. chives, parsley, or as a sweet dish with the addition of a little sugar and flavouring, or fresh fruits.

KIPPER CHEESE SOUFFLÉ

&

2 hard-boiled eggs	30 g/1 oz/4 tbsp flour
225 g/½ lb kippers	280 ml/½ pint/1¼ cups milk
2 tbsp cream	3 eggs, separated
salt and freshly ground black pepper	55 g/2 oz/½ cup freshly grated Cheddar cheese
30 g/1 oz/2 tbsp butter	

Put the boiled eggs and the kippers into a food processor and blend at low speed until smooth. Transfer to a bowl and add the cream, mix well and season. Spoon the mixture into a greased soufflé dish. Melt the butter in a saucepan, add the flour and cook for 1 minute, gradually stir in the milk and bring to the boil. Lower the heat and cook until thickened, while continuing to stir. Remove from the heat. Gradually beat the egg yolks into the sauce, sprinkle in the cheese, season and mix well. Whisk the egg whites until stiff, and fold into the sauce. Pour over the kippers in the soufflé dish and bake in a preheated fairly hot oven (190°C/375°F/Gas 5) for 30 minutes until well risen and golden brown. Serve immediately.

SPANISH OMELET

2 tbsp olive oil
2 large potatoes, peeled and sliced
2 onions, peeled and thinly sliced
6 eggs

salt and freshly ground black
 pepper
finely chopped chives to garnish

Heat some of the oil in a frying pan, add the potatoes and cook lightly until golden brown. Remove from the pan, add the onions to the pan and cook gently until soft. Remove from the pan. Drain the potatoes and onions on kitchen paper. Beat the eggs in a bowl, add the potatoes and the onions and season. Heat the remaining oil in the frying pan, add the egg and potato mix and cook until the edges of the omelet are set. Turn out on to a plate, then reverse into the pan and allow the other side to brown. Turn on to a warm serving dish, cut into four wedges and sprinkle with the chives.

EGGS MORNAY

55 g/2 oz/4 tbsp butter
55 g/2 oz/½ cup flour
575 ml/1 pint/2½ cups milk
150 ml/¼ pint/⅔ cup cream
1 tsp made mustard (US prepared
 mustard)

110 g/4 oz/1 cup grated cheese
salt and freshly ground black
 pepper
6 hard-boiled eggs, shelled
110 g/4 oz/¾ cup diced cooked ham

Melt the butter in a saucepan, stir in the flour and cook for 2 minutes. Add the milk gradually and, continuing to whisk, bring to the boil until thickened. Remove from the heat, add the cream and the mustard with half of the cheese to the prepared sauce, mix well and season. Cut the eggs in half lengthwise, coat the bottom of an ovenproof dish with some of the sauce and place the halved eggs on top, cut side down. Sprinkle the diced ham on top of the eggs and pour the remaining sauce over. Sprinkle the remaining cheese over the top, and heat in a preheated moderate oven (180°C/ 350°F/Gas 4) for about 10 minutes. Put under the grill to brown the top just before serving.

MONICA'S HAM AND CHEESE QUICHE

———————— ❧ ————————

Shortcrust pastry

170 g/6 oz/1½ cups flour   pinch of salt
75 g/3 oz/6 tbsp margarine   water to mix

Make the pastry as instructed on page 101.

Filling

110 g/4 oz/¾ cup diced ham *or* lean
  bacon, cooked
1 spring onion, peeled and finely
  chopped
75 g/3 oz/¾ cup grated Cheddar
  cheese
3 eggs

280 ml/½ pint/1¼ cups milk
salt and freshly ground black
  pepper
pinch of nutmeg
½ tbsp chopped parsley to garnish

Roll out the pastry, and use to line a 20 cm/8 inch flan (pie) dish. Bake blind (page 131). Put the ham, the onion and half the cheese into the pastry case and spread evenly over the bottom. Beat the eggs and the milk together, season and pour into the case and mix well. Top with the remaining cheese and sprinkle with nutmeg. Bake in a preheated warm oven (170°C/ 325°F/Gas 3) for 30 minutes, until set and golden. Sprinkle the chopped parsley on top before serving.

LEEK AND TOMATO QUICHE

———————— ❧ ————————

Shortcrust pastry

170 g/6 oz/1½ cups flour   pinch of salt
75 g/3 oz/6 tbsp margarine   water to mix

Make the pastry as instructed on page 101.

Sister Benedict working with the cattle

Filling

30 g/1 oz/2 tbsp butter

1 leek, trimmed and thinly sliced
  using only a little of the green

3 eggs

150 ml/¼ pint/⅔ cup milk

150 ml/¼ pint/⅔ cup cream

salt and freshly ground black
  pepper

30 g/1 oz/¼ cup grated Cheddar
  cheese

2 medium-sized tomatoes, sliced

2 tsp chopped parsley

Line a 20 cm/8 inch quiche dish with the pastry and bake blind (page 131). Heat the butter in a frying pan and sweat the leek until soft. Beat the eggs, add the milk and the cream, and season. Place the leeks on the pastry, and sprinkle over with the cheese. Place the tomatoes on top, and pour over the egg mixture. Bake in a preheated warm oven (170°C/325°F/Gas 3) for 30 minutes. Sprinkle with the chopped parsley before serving.

SPINACH CHEESE FLAN

450 g/1 lb fresh spinach *or* 225 g/
  8 oz frozen spinach

225 g/8 oz/1⅓ cups cottage cheese

55 g/2 oz/½ cup grated Cheddar
  cheese

2 eggs

150 ml/¼ pint/⅔ cup milk

salt and pepper

freshly grated nutmeg

170 g/6 oz puff pastry (we use a
  commercial variety)

Roll out the pastry and line a 20 cm/8 inch flan dish.

Wash the spinach, remove and discard the stalks. Put the spinach into a saucepan, cover tightly and cook over a very low heat for about 5 minutes. Drain well and press until almost dry. (Cook frozen spinach according to the directions given on the packet.)

Chop the spinach finely, or you could give it a quick whizz in a blender, but avoid turning it into a purée. Place the spinach in a bowl with the cottage and Cheddar cheese, and mix. Beat the eggs, add to the cheese and spinach, mix and season. Pour the mixture into the flan dish, sprinkle with nutmeg and bake in a preheated fairly hot oven (190°C/375°F/Gas 5) for 30 minutes until golden brown and set.

MACARONI CHEESE

110 g/4 oz macaroni
55 g/2 oz/4 tbsp butter
55 g/2 oz/½ cup flour
575 ml/1 pint/2½ cups milk *or* three-quarters milk and one-quarter cream

salt and pepper
225 g/8 oz/2 cups grated Cheddar cheese
1 tsp made mustard (US prepared mustard)

Put the macaroni into boiling salted water and boil briskly until cooked, 10–15 minutes. Strain and rinse well.

Melt butter in a saucepan, stir in the flour and cook gently for 1 minute. Add the milk gradually; simmer while continuing to whisk, until the sauce has thickened. Remove from the heat, season and add 140 g/5 oz/1¼ cups of the grated cheese, mustard and macaroni. Mix the ingredients gently and put into an ovenproof dish. Sprinkle the remaining cheese on top. Bake in a preheated oven (180°C/350°F/Gas 4) for 20 minutes, until the dish is heated through and the cheese has melted.

CURRIED EGGS

30 g/1 oz/2 tbsp margarine *or* butter
1 small onion, peeled and finely chopped
½ sweet apple, peeled and finely chopped
2 tsp curry powder
2 tsp tomato paste
30 g/1 oz/4 tbsp flour

280 ml/½ pint/1¼ cups chicken stock
30 g/1 oz/2 tbsp sultanas
30 g/1 oz/¼ cup ground almonds
1 tbsp chutney
salt
8 eggs
½ tsp paprika
boiled rice to serve

Melt the margarine in a saucepan and sweat the onion and apple slowly for 2 minutes. Add the curry powder and tomato paste and continue to cook gently for a further 2 minutes. Mix in the flour and gradually add the chicken stock whilst continuing to stir. Simmer gently for a further 20–25 minutes, then blend on low speed until smooth. Return to the pan and add the sultanas, almonds, chutney and seasoning.

While the sauce is cooking, put the eggs into boiling water, bring back to the boil and boil gently for 12 minutes. Plunge into cold water for 1 minute and shell. Slice the eggs lengthwise, place on a heated serving dish, coat with sauce, sprinkle a little paprika on top, and serve with boiled rice.

Sister Benedict displaying the day's newly laid eggs

The cows coming home

SUPPER DISHES

✤

*V*espers at six o'clock marks the close of the day's toil. From the classroom, kitchen, office, farm, shop and all their various activities, the Nuns gather in their Chapel and join together in thanking God. Freed from the cares of the day, tranquillity envelopes the Community as they gather in their refectory for their evening meal. Unlike their main meal at midday, the atmosphere is one of relaxation, as the Nuns chat and comment on their day while enjoying a light simple meal. The evening meal, or supper, in the past consisted mainly of either eggs or cheese, except on occasions of celebration, such as important feast days, when it was customary to have a special 'treat'.

Suppers today, though still a very simple meal, take full advantage of a wider range of ingredients to provide interest and variety.

RED CABBAGE, BACON AND APPLE FRY

half a head of red cabbage
6 streaky rashers
1 tbsp vegetable oil
30 g/1 oz/2 tbsp butter

2 onions, peeled and sliced
2 medium cooking apples, cored, peeled and sliced
salt and freshly ground black pepper

Discard the outer leaves of the cabbage, cut the head into quarters, remove the stalk and shred thinly. Cut the rashers into thin strips. Heat the oil in a frying pan and slowly cook the rashers and the onions, then add the cabbage and the apples. Reduce the heat, put a lid or large plate on top of the frying pan and cook gently for 10 minutes, stirring occasionally. The cabbage should have a bite at this point. Do not overcook. Check seasoning, and serve immediately in deep plates or bowls with brown bread and butter.

COURGETTE LASAGNE

&

1 tbsp oil

1 onion, peeled and sliced

1 red pepper, peeled, sliced and deseeded

1 carrot, peeled and cut into julienne strips

450 g/1 lb courgettes, washed and sliced

2 cloves of garlic, crushed

335 g/12 oz tinned tomatoes

1 tsp tomato purée

1 tsp chopped fresh basil

salt and freshly ground pepper

1 tsp sugar

110 g/4 oz/½ cup cream cheese

55 g/2 oz/½ cup grated Cheddar cheese

170 g/6 oz lasagne (Easy-cook)

475 ml/16 fl oz/2 cups white sauce (page 131)

30 g/1 oz/3 tbsp freshly grated Parmesan cheese

Heat the oil in a pan and gently cook the onion, pepper and carrot for 2 minutes. Add the courgettes and continue to cook for a further 2–3 minutes. Then add the remaining ingredients, seasoning and sugar.

Mix the cream cheese and Cheddar cheese together. In an ovenproof dish, layer the courgette mix, the lasagne sheets and cheese, ending with the courgettes. Pour over the white sauce and sprinkle with Parmesan. Bake in a preheated oven (190°C/375°F/Gas 5) for 30 minutes.

SISTER DOROTHY'S SALMON POTATO PIE

&

425 g/15 oz tinned salmon

280 ml/½ pint/1¼ cups white sauce — fairly thick (page 131)

salt and freshly ground black pepper

1 small onion, finely chopped

75 g/3 oz/6 tbsp butter

900 g/2 lb warm mashed potatoes

Remove the skin and bone from the salmon and flake into small pieces, mix into the white sauce and season. Add the chopped onion and the butter to the potatoes, mix well and season. Line a greased pie dish with some of the potatoes, place the salmon on top and cover with the remaining potatoes.

Score the top with a fork and put in a hot oven (220°C/425°F/Gas 7) for 15 minutes to heat through. Serve with a dish of peas.

Sister Dorothy recalls this recipe from her childhood in Tipperary. It was frequently made by her late mother and was a great family favourite, particularly with the younger children.

MUSSEL RISOTTO

———————— ❧ ————————

1 onion, peeled and sliced

110 g/4 oz/½ cup butter

225 g/8 oz/1⅓ cups risotto rice

280 ml/½ pint/1¼ cups chicken stock

900 g/2 lb mussels, cooked and shelled

1 clove of garlic, crushed

salt and freshly ground black pepper

1 tbsp chopped parsley to garnish

Sweat the onion in 30 g/1 oz/2 tbsp butter but do not brown. Add the rice and cook for 2 minutes, add half the stock and allow to cook very slowly for a few minutes. Add the remainder of the stock and continue to cook very slowly until the stock is absorbed and the rice is cooked; this will take about 20 minutes. At this point add the mussels, the garlic and the rest of the butter. Season, sprinkle with the chopped parsley and serve piled high on a warm dish.

BEAN AND VEGETABLE CASSEROLE

———————— ❧ ————————

75 g/3 oz/½ cup haricot beans

170 g/6 oz/1¼ cups black eyed beans

3 tbsp olive oil

2 medium onions, peeled and sliced

1 leek, trimmed and sliced

2 cloves of garlic, peeled and crushed

3 medium carrots, scraped and sliced

2 peppers — 1 green and 1 yellow, deseeded and sliced

2 sticks of celery, trimmed, washed and sliced

3 tomatoes, quartered

2 x 396 g/14 oz tins tomatoes

bouquet garni (parsley, thyme, bay leaf)

salt and freshly ground black pepper

The Sisters gather for a song.

An evening stroll in the grounds

Soak the beans in cold water overnight. Drain and rinse well in cold water. Put into a saucepan, cover with water, bring to the boil and simmer for 20 minutes or until tender; drain and rinse. Heat the oil in a saucepan and sweat the onions, leek and garlic until soft but not brown. Add the carrots, peppers and celery and continue to sweat for a further 10 minutes. Add the tomatoes, fresh and canned, and the bouquet garni. Season and cook gently for 20 minutes; add a little water if necessary. Add the beans, mix well and continue to simmer for a further 5–10 minutes. The vegetables should have a bite and must not be allowed to overcook. Serve with pasta and a salad.

This is a colourful and very flavoursome vegetable stew. It is very popular in the Kylemore Abbey Restaurant and merited a special mention in the Egon Ronay Guide.

PASTA WITH TOMATOES AND BASIL

675 g/1½ lb Irish *or* beef tomatoes
3 cloves of garlic, peeled
3 tbsp fresh basil

450 g/1 lb bow pasta
salt and freshly ground black
  pepper
90 ml/3 fl oz/⅓ cup olive oil

Skin the tomatoes, remove the seeds (page 131) and chop the flesh into small pieces. Finely chop the garlic, and tear the basil into small pieces. Cook the pasta in seasoned water, to which you have added a little oil; strain into a colander and drain well. Put all the other ingredients into a large warmed serving bowl, add the hot pasta, mix and serve immediately.

This very simple pasta recipe is dependent upon using first-class ingredients, top quality olive oil, freshly picked basil and tomatoes likewise, if possible. You won't believe how good it is at the right time of year.

GOOSE BLACK PUDDING

As Mrs Beeton would say, first kill your goose — or two ducks would do. The correct way is to cut the goose just behind the head and collect the blood as it flows out.

For every 575 ml/1 pint/2½ cups of blood, add 55 g/2 oz/½ cup of oatmeal, a generous sprinkling of pepper, salt and allspice. Mix together and bake in a moderate oven (180°C/350°F/Gas 4) until solid. Before serving, cut into squares and fry gently in oil and butter.

This is Sister Benedict's recollection of a supper dish that would be served on the day of goose-killing. Other recollections suggest that thyme and onion would be added to the blood for extra flavour — in the unlikely event that the reader wants to try!

HAM SOUFFLÉ

55 g/2 oz/4 tbsp butter
110 g/¼ lb mushrooms, chopped
110 g/¼ lb cooked ham, finely
   chopped
575 ml/1 pint/2½ cups milk

salt and freshly ground black
   pepper
pinch of nutmeg
55 g/2 oz/½ cup flour
5 eggs, separated

Melt 30 g/1 oz/2 tbsp butter, add the mushrooms and cook gently for a few minutes. Chop the ham finely and add to the mushrooms. Season the milk with salt, pepper and nutmeg and bring to the boil. Melt the remaining butter and gradually add in the flour. Cook for 1 minute. Add the milk slowly to the saucepan, stirring constantly until thickened. Remove from the heat and add the egg yolks, one at a time, blending well before the addition of another. Add the ham and mushrooms to the sauce and mix well. Beat the egg whites until stiff, fold into the ham and mushroom mixture. Spoon into a buttered soufflé dish and bake in a fairly hot oven (200°C/400°F/Gas 6) for 20 minutes. Serve immediately.

TOAD IN THE HOLE

225 g/½ lb/2 cups flour
1 tsp salt
2 eggs

575 ml/1 pint/2½ cups milk
450 g/1 lb sausages
2 tbsp dripping *or* oil

Sieve the flour and salt into a bowl. Make a well in the centre and drop the eggs into it. Add the milk gradually and mix to a smooth batter. Leave to stand for 1–2 hours.

Fry the sausages lightly. Melt the fat and put into a shallow ovenproof dish. Place the sausages in the dish, at even intervals, and pour the batter over them. Bake in a preheated oven (200°C/400°F/Gas 6) until the batter has risen well and is brown — 40 minutes. Cut into a large square and serve straight from the oven.

STUFFED PEPPERS

4 good-sized green peppers

170 g/6 oz/¾ cup cooked brown rice

75 g/3 oz ham, chopped very small

1 small onion, finely chopped

55 g/2 oz/⅓ cup raisins

55 g/2 oz/½ cup nuts, chopped

a little chopped parsley

75 g/3 oz/¾ cup grated cheese

salt and freshly ground black pepper

1 tsp prepared mustard

280 ml/½ pint/1¼ cups white sauce (page 131)

Remove the stems from the peppers, cut in halves lengthwise and scoop out the seeds. Put into boiling salted water and simmer for 10 minutes. Remove from the pan and drain.

Mix together in a bowl the rice, ham, onion, raisins, nuts, parsley and half the cheese. Add seasoning to taste. Fill the pepper halves with the rice mixture, place in an ovenproof dish and cover with foil. Bake in a preheated moderate oven (180°C/ 350°F/Gas 4) for 30 minutes.

Meanwhile, add a little of the remaining cheese and the mustard to the white sauce and mix well. Remove the foil from the cooked peppers, coat with the white sauce, sprinkle cheese on top and return it to the oven until the cheese is bubbly. Or, if you prefer, put it under a hot grill for a few minutes. Serve immediately.

Benedictine Hospitality

*I*n both the Old and New Testaments, the concept of hospitality as part of a godly life is etched clear. It is not surprising then, that the father of Western monasticism, when fleeing for solitude, and faced with a constant and turbulent host of troubled or curious folk (see The Dialogues of St Gregory — the definitive 'life' of St Benedict), decided that to pilgrims and guests must be shown special attention, all must 'be received as Christ Himself'. This dramatic and all-embracing statement is a challenge that all monastics must strive to meet.

In our Monastery at Kylemore, the constant flow of visitors, tourists, schoolgirls, and yes, pilgrims, allows us to try and live out this challenge every day of every year. In this cookbook, you will sample many of the recipes tried and tested both on our visitors and on our boarding students.

Sharing the Bread of Life daily, we know that nourishment for the journey of life is also a visible sign of solidarity between one person and the next.

Peace and a gentle unity pervade the table. The monastics serve one another according to the guidance of St Benedict, showing a reverence and joy in the action that reflects the graciousness of the Lord.

All things considered, this should be a different kind of cookbook. It too should be pervaded by the spirit of peace — and good fellowship!

Breads and Cakes

✦

*B*read-making and home-baking in Kylemore Abbey revolve around Sisters Benedict and Bernard — the two Sister B's — who continue the tradition of this gentle art. Their predecessors Sisters Bernadette, Ita and Dymphna today enjoy a peaceful and happy older life, where the bread is made by other hands.

The smell of freshly baked bread is part of the Abbey kitchen, and of the hospitality associated with the Community. Much of today's baking has its origin in traditional recipes, but with the rapid growth in tourist-related activities, the baking repertoire has expanded dramatically to include some innovative ideas. The two Sister B's are constantly experimenting, while at the same time retaining the essence and integrity of real food. It is for this reason so many of the visitors to Kylemore Abbey seek advice on the making of quite simple fare, such as wheaten or sultana scones. We attempt in this section to include a selection of that which is simple and good.

Long may the two Sister B's continue to do what they do so well. We dedicate this section to Sisters Bernadette, Ita and Dymphna, and their predecessors.

Sadly Sister Bernadette has passed away since writing this. We mourn her passing and she will be long remembered.

CATHLEEN'S BROWN BREAD

⸙

450 g/1 lb/4 cups white flour
450 g/1 lb/4 cups wholemeal flour
  (US wholewheat flour)
2 tsp bread soda (US baking soda)
2 tsp salt
55 g/2 oz/¾ cup wheat bran

30 g/1 oz wheatgerm
55 g/2 oz oatmeal
2 eggs
1 litre/1¾ pints/4½ cups buttermilk
  or 150 ml/¼ pint/⅔ cup natural
  yoghurt mixed with 900 ml/1½
  pints/3¾ cups buttermilk

Sieve the white flour, wholemeal flour, bread soda and salt into a bowl, add to the bowl any wholemeal flour that has not gone through the sieve. Add the bran, wheatgerm and oatmeal, and mix well. Beat the eggs and the buttermilk together. Add the liquid to the dry ingredients and mix to a loose dough. Put into three 450 g/1 lb well-greased loaf tins/pans, and bake in a preheated warm oven (200°C/400°F/Gas 6) for 40–45 minutes. Turn out and cool on a wire tray.

SISTER BERNARD'S BROWN BREAD

225 g/½ lb/2 cups white flour

1 tsp bread soda (US baking soda)

½ tsp salt

450 g/1 lb/4 cups wholemeal flour (US wholewheat flour)

75 g/3 oz/1 cup wheat bran

15 g/½ oz wheatgerm

30 g/1 oz/⅓ cup pinhead oatmeal

1 egg

575 ml/1 pint/2½ cups buttermilk

½ tbsp treacle (US molasses)

Sieve the white flour, bread soda and salt into a bowl, and add all the other dry ingredients. Beat the egg, add to the buttermilk and mix in the treacle. Add the liquid to the dry ingredients, mix to a soft dough, and divide into two well-greased 450 g/1 lb loaf tins/pans. Bake in a preheated warm oven (200°C/400°F/Gas 6) for 45 minutes. Turn out and cool on a wire tray.

SISTER DYMPHNA'S RAISIN SODA BREAD

(or Sweet Cake)

450 g/1 lb/4 cups flour

1 tsp salt

1 tsp bread soda (US baking soda)

55 g/2 oz/4 tbsp sugar

110 g/4 oz/⅔ cup raisins

350 ml/12 fl oz/1½ cups sour milk

Sieve the flour, salt and bread soda into a bowl. Add the sugar and the raisins, mix with enough sour milk to make a stiff dough and knead lightly. Turn out on to a floured board and flatten into a round shape. Put on to a floured baking sheet, cut a deep cross on top and bake in a preheated warm oven (200°C/400°F/Gas 6) for 45 minutes. Test by tapping the bottom of the bread; if it sounds hollow, it is cooked.

This bread is also known as 'blessed bread'. It is traditional in the Monastery to bless a freshly baked loaf of this bread on St Agatha's Day, 5 February, each year.

SISTER AIDAN'S SODA FARLS

——————— ❧ ———————

225 g/½ lb/2 cups plain flour
1 level tsp bread soda (US baking soda)

¼ tsp salt
150 ml/¼ pint/⅔ cup buttermilk

Sieve the flour and bread soda into a bowl and add the salt. Mix with the buttermilk and knead to a soft dough. Turn out on to a floured board and shape into a round 1.2 cm/½ inch thick. Cut into triangles and bake on a griddle for 8 minutes on each side. Eat straight from the griddle with lots of butter.

Sister Aidan likes the farls split and fried on the pan in butter or bacon fat.

MRS RUDDY'S BOXTY

——————— ❧ ———————

110 g/4 oz/1 cup self-raising flour
110 g/4 oz/1 cup plain flour
75 g/3 oz/6 tbsp margarine
75 g/3 oz bacon fat
1 tsp salt

1 tsp sugar (if liked)
225 g/½ lb grated raw potato
110 g/4 oz cooked and mashed potato
a little buttermilk

Put the flours into a mixing bowl, rub in the margarine and fat, add the salt and sugar. Wash, peel, rinse and dry the potatoes, then grate, but not too finely. Put into a clean cotton cloth and squeeze out the juice. Add the raw and mashed potato, mix well and add a little buttermilk, or a little juice of raw potato if necessary, to form a stiff dough. Roll out to about 2.5 cm/1 inch, cut into rounds and place on a greased baking sheet. Cook in a preheated moderate oven (180°C/350°F/ Gas 4) for about 40 minutes. Serve warm, generously spread with butter.

As a younger woman, Mrs Ruddy helped with the cooking in the Kylemore Abbey kitchen. We are grateful for her recipe from those days.

Sister Bernard, 'the baking nun', in the kitchen

Mrs Kathleen Ruddy, now in her eighties, who worked with the nuns for many years

PLAIN BROWN YEAST BREAD

———————— ❧ ————————

(Our Daily Bread)

1 tsp brown sugar

850 ml/1½ pints/3½ cups tepid
milk and water — equal parts

20 g/¾ oz fresh yeast (if using
dried yeast, follow the packet
instructions)

335 g/12 oz/3 cups wholemeal flour
(US wholewheat flour)

335 g/12 oz/3 cups white flour

pinch of salt

Dissolve the sugar in a little of the warm liquid and stir in the yeast. Leave
to stand in a warm place until frothy; add the remaining liquid. Sieve the
flour and salt into a large mixing bowl, adding any wholemeal that has not
gone through the sieve. Make a well in the centre and pour in the yeast
liquid. Mix to a soft dough. Turn out on to a floured board and knead well
for a few minutes until very smooth and shiny. Return the dough to the
bowl, cover with a tea towel and leave to stand in a warm part of the kitchen
until it has doubled in size.

Turn the dough out on to a floured board and knock back to its original
size. Divide the dough in two and put into three well-greased one-pound
tins/pans, and leave once again to rise in a warm area of the kitchen, covered
with a tea towel. When they have doubled in size, bake in a preheated oven
(200°C/400°F/Gas 6) for 20–30 minutes. The bread is cooked if it sounds
hollow when tapped underneath. Remove from the tins/pans and cool on a
wire tray.

PLAIN WHITE YEAST BREAD

———————— ❧ ————————

1 tsp sugar

280 ml/½ pint/1¼ cups tepid water,
or milk and water — equal parts

15 g/½ oz fresh yeast (if using
dried yeast, follow the packet
instructions)

450 g/1 lb/4 cups strong white
flour

pinch of salt

Dissolve the sugar in a little of the warm liquid, stir in the yeast and leave to
stand in a warm place until frothy. Add the remaining liquid. Sieve the flour

and the salt into a large mixing bowl. Make a well in the centre, pour in the yeast liquid and mix to a soft dough. Turn out on to a floured board and knead well until very smooth and shiny. Return the dough to the bowl, cover with a tea towel and leave to stand in a warm part of the kitchen until it has doubled in size. This will take about 1 hour.

Turn the dough out on to a floured board and knock back to its original size. Divide the dough in two and put into two well-greased one-pound loaf tins/pans, and leave once again to rise in a warm area of the kitchen, covered with a tea towel. When it has doubled in size, bake in a preheated fairly hot oven (200°C/400°F/Gas 6) for 20–30 minutes. The bread is cooked if it sounds hollow when tapped underneath. Remove from the tins/pans and cool on a wire tray.

TOMATO AND SPRING ONION YEAST BREAD

1 tsp sugar

15 g/½ oz fresh yeast (if using dried yeast, follow instructions)

280 ml/½ pint/1¼ cups tepid water *or* half water and half milk

450 g/1 lb/4 cups strong white flour

pinch of salt

2 large tomatoes, skinned and chopped

4 spring onions, trimmed, washed and finely chopped

Make as for Plain White Yeast Bread (above). The tomatoes and onions are added to the dough at knock back stage. To do this, flatten the dough, sprinkle the tomatoes and onions on top, and fold in by kneading. Then proceed as for Plain White Yeast Bread.

SISTER BERNADETTE'S WHEATEN SCONES

140 g/5 oz/1¼ cups white flour

1 tsp bread soda (US baking soda)

¼ tsp baking powder

½ tsp salt

280 g/10 oz/2½ cups wholemeal flour (US wholewheat flour)

1 tsp sugar

55 g/2 oz/4 tbsp margarine

2 eggs, beaten (reserve a little to brush over the scones)

280 ml/½ pint/1¼ cups buttermilk

Sieve the white flour, bread soda, baking powder and salt into a bowl. Add the wholemeal and the sugar and rub in the margarine. Mix the eggs with the buttermilk, make a well in the centre of the flour, add the eggs and milk, and mix to a soft dough. Turn out on to a floured board, and roll out to about 2.5 cm/1 inch thick. Cut into triangles and brush over with a little beaten egg. Put on to a greased baking sheet and bake in a preheated oven (200°C/400°F/Gas 6) for 15–20 minutes. Cool on a wire tray.

SISTER ITA'S SULTANA SCONES

450 g/1 lb/4 cups flour
1½ tsp baking powder
½ tsp salt
55 g/2 oz/4 tbsp margarine
55 g/2 oz/4 tbsp sugar

110 g/4 oz/⅔ cup sultanas (US golden raisins)
15 g/½ oz mixed peel (US candied citrus peel) (optional)
2 eggs
280 ml/½ pint/1¼ cups milk

Sieve the flour, bread soda, baking powder and the salt into a bowl, and rub in the margarine. Add the sugar, fruit and the peel, if using. Mix well. Beat the eggs and mix with the milk, reserving a little to brush over the scones. Make a well in the centre of the flour, add the eggs and milk and mix to a soft dough. Turn out on to a floured board and roll out to about 2.5 cm/ 1 inch thick. Cut into rounds, using a 6.3 cm/2½ inch fluted cutter. Brush over with some beaten egg. Put on to a greased baking sheet and bake in a preheated hot oven (200°C/400°F/Gas 6) for 15–20 minutes. Turn out on to a wire tray to cool.

From the days of the Abbey Guest House of the 1950s to the tour buses of the 1990s, and right up to her retirement a few years ago at the age of 90, Sister Ita's scones were legendary in Connemara. She is sadly missed by visitors, drivers and guides who fondly recall her friendship and warm hospitality.

ROCK BUNS

450 g/1 lb/4 cups flour

¼ tsp salt

2 tsp baking powder

140 g/5 oz/½ cup butter *or* margarine

110 g/4 oz/½ cup caster sugar (US superfine sugar)

140 g/5 oz/¾ cup mixed dried fruit (US light and dark raisins, currants)

30 g/1 oz/¼ cup mixed peel (US candied citrus peel)

2 eggs

280 ml/½ pint/1¼ cups milk

Sieve the flour, salt and the baking powder into a bowl, rub in the butter, and add the sugar, fruit and the mixed peel. Beat the eggs, reserving a little to brush over the buns. Make a well in the centre of the flour, add the beaten eggs and enough milk to make a soft dough. Using 2 forks, place the mixture in rough mounds on a greased baking sheet. Brush with a little beaten egg and bake in a preheated oven (200°C/400°F/Gas 6) for 15–20 minutes. Place on a wire tray to cool.

For a variation of this recipe, instead of mixed fruit use:

75 g/3 oz/⅓ cup glacé cherries (US candied cherries) cut small

45 g/1½ oz/⅓ cup mixed peel (US candied citrus peel)

Feast Days

*T*he traditional celebration of Saints Days brings a delightful opportunity to break with the monotony of the monastic diet. Since every Sister keeps her patronal feast, and when finally professed her profession anniversary, there is ample scope for culinary novelty.

Besides the great feasts of Easter and Christmas, such important festivals as Holy Cross, All Saints, Michaelmas, Candlemas, Ascension Day, Corpus Christi, Pentecost, and the Benedictine days of 10 February for St Scholastica, 21 March and 11 July for St Benedict, bring with them special treats for the Community.

The Monastic Profession

*T*he Christian consecration of Baptism shared by all is celebrated by a Christening Feast and the following years with a birthday of that feast. Once professed, this is repeated with a feast of the Profession Day which takes place on the anniversary of the day on which the final three vows were taken.

Solemn profession of these vows is made publicly in the Abbey Church in the presence of the Archbishop or his representative, and of the whole Community and the family and friends of the professed. To promise 'forever', Conversion of Life, Stability and Obedience is an awesome thing. Even those who are simply on-lookers are moved by the enormity of the promise made by the newly professed.

The meal which follows is similar to any bridal banquet and just as exciting!

The Clothing Day

*T*he day that a Novice receives her habit is another day of festivity for the Community. The Clothing Cake will appear at supper, along with other treats, as the cooks discover the new Sister's preference.

The celebratory meal is a supper which follows directly after Vespers (Evening Prayer). The cake for this celebration is a rich fruit cake. The festival sharing of a Community is much more than a laden table. It is the exchange of affirmation of peace and love.

KYLEMORE PROFESSION CAKE

————— ❧ —————

900 g/2 lbs/5 cups dried mixed
  fruit — raisins, sultanas, currants
110 g/4 oz prunes, chopped
110 g/4 oz dates, chopped
110 g/4 oz/1 cup chopped
  unblanched almonds
110 g/4 oz/1 cup ground almonds
110 g/4 oz/½ cup glacé cherries
  (US candied cherries)

½ apple, grated
grated rind of ½ lemon
½ tsp mixed spice
250 g/9 oz/1 cup *plus* 2 tbsp butter
250 g/9 oz/1 cup *plus* 1 tbsp sugar
310 g/11 oz/2¾ cups flour
6 eggs

Grease a 23 cm/9 inch round cake tin/pan and line with 2 layers of greaseproof paper (US parchment paper).

Mix the dried fruit, dates, chopped almonds, cherries, grated apple, lemon rind and the mixed spice together in a bowl. Cream the butter and the sugar in a large bowl until light and fluffy. Sieve the flour and beat the eggs. Add the beaten eggs gradually to the creamed butter and sugar, beating well between additions. Fold in the sieved flour, and finally add in the fruit, making sure it is well distributed. Mix thoroughly. Put the mixture into the prepared tin/pan, and bake in a preheated warm oven (160°C/325°F/Gas 3) for the first hour. Lower the temperature to a very cool oven (140°C/275°F/Gas 1) for a further 2½–3 hours. Test with a skewer to ensure that the cake is cooked. Allow to cool before removing from the tin/pan. Store in an airtight tin until ready to ice.

Final Profession takes place after seven years, with the taking of final solemn vows, receiving the ring and the cowl, and the making of life's commitment. It is a day of great joy and celebration in the presence of the entire Community, family and close relatives.
And for the 50th Anniversary of First Profession, the Golden Jubilee, this is also the celebration cake.

SUNDAY FRUIT CAKE

— ❧ —

225 g/8 oz/2 cups self-raising flour

170 g/6 oz/¾ cup margarine

170 g/6 oz/¾ cup caster sugar (US superfine sugar)

grated rind of 1 lemon

4 eggs

110 g/4 oz/⅔ cup sultanas (US golden raisins)

55 g/2 oz/½ cup chopped almonds

55 g/2 oz/½ cup candied peel (US candied citrus peel)

55 g/2 oz/¼ cup glacé cherries (US candied cherries)

Grease a 20 cm/8 inch round cake tin/pan and line with greaseproof paper (US parchment paper). Sieve the flour. Cream the margarine, sugar and the lemon rind in a large bowl until light and fluffy. Add the eggs one at a time, beating well between each addition. Toss the sultanas, almonds, candied peel and the cherries in a little of the flour and add to the cake mixture. Add the flour all at once and fold in gently. Put mixture into the prepared tin/pan and bake in a preheated very cool oven (140°C/275°F/Gas 1) for 2–2½ hours. Test with a skewer to ensure the cake is cooked, and leave to cool in the tin/pan before turning out.

VISITORS' FRUIT CAKE

— ❧ —

250 g/9 oz/2¼ cups flour

1 tsp ground mixed spice

900 g/2 lb/5 cups mixed dried fruit (US light and dark raisins, currants)

225 g/8 oz/½ cup cherries

225 g/8 oz/1 cup butter

200 g/7 oz/1 cup sugar

5 eggs, beaten

Line a 20 cm/8 inch cake tin/pan with greaseproof paper (US parchment paper). Sieve the flour and the spice into a bowl. Combine the mixed fruit and the cherries. Cream the butter and the sugar until light and fluffy. Add the eggs gradually to the mixture, beating well between additions. Fold in the flour and add the mixed fruit and cherries. Put the mixture into the prepared tin/pan and bake in a preheated very cool oven (150°C/300°F/ Gas 2) for 2 hours. Test with a skewer to ensure the cake is cooked, and cool before removing from the tin/pan.

The counter area in the Restaurant showing the rich selection of cakes and bread

Sister Bernard making bread

ABBEY SPONGE CAKE

———————————— ❧ ————————————

110 g/4 oz/1 cup flour

110 g/4 oz/½ cup caster sugar
(US superfine sugar)

4 eggs

Filling

2 tbsp home-made jam, any variety
but raspberry is best

200 ml/7 fl oz/¾ cup whipped
cream

or

lemon curd (page 101) with whipped cream

or

fresh berries — raspberries, strawberries, blackberries — lightly mashed with
a little caster sugar and folded into whipped cream

Grease two 23 cm/9 inch sandwich tins (US round cake pans), and dust with a little flour and caster sugar. Sieve the flour. Separate the whites of the eggs from the yolks. Put the whites into a clean, dry bowl. Add the sugar to the yolks and whisk with an electric mixer until light and thickened. Whisk the egg whites until stiff and fold into the yolk mixture. Very gently fold the flour into the eggs. Spoon the mixture into the prepared tins/pans and bake in a preheated fairly hot oven (190°C/375°F/Gas 5) for 20 minutes. Turn out the tins/pans and leave to cool on a wire tray. When cool, spread one sponge with the filling of your choice and sandwich with the second sponge. If using jam or curd, heat it very slightly and spread on each side of the sandwich with the cream in the centre. Sprinkle with caster sugar and serve.

SISTER KAROL'S CHOCOLATE RASPBERRY SANDWICH

———————————— ❧ ————————————

(All-in-one method)

225 g/½ lb/2 cups flour
1 tsp baking powder
45 g/1½ oz chocolate powder

4 eggs
170 g/6 oz/¾ cup caster sugar (US
superfine sugar)
170 g/6 oz/¾ cup butter

Filling

75 g/3 oz/6 tbsp butter

75 g/3 oz/⅔ cup icing sugar (US powdered sugar)

1 tbsp milk

2 tbsp raspberry essence

For the cake: Sieve the flour, baking powder and chocolate powder into a bowl. Add all the other ingredients and beat with a wooden spoon until the mixture is soft and creamy. Use a blender or food processor if preferred.

Divide the mixture into two well-greased 20 cm/8 inch sandwich tins (US round cake pans), and bake in a preheated oven (170°C/325°F/Gas 3) for 25 minutes. Turn out on to a wire tray to cool.

For the filling: Mix all ingredients into a bowl and beat until light and creamy.

When the sandwich is cold, spread one half with filling; place the other half on top and press the cakes together gently. Dredge the top with a little caster sugar.

CHOCOLATE CAKE

225 g/½ lb/2 cups flour

½ tsp bread soda (US baking soda)

½ tsp baking powder

55 g/2 oz cocoa

pinch of salt

170 g/6 oz/¾ cup brown sugar

75 g/3 oz/3 tbsp golden syrup

150 ml/¼ pint/⅔ cup milk

150 ml/¼ pint/⅔ cup oil

1 egg, beaten

55 g/2 oz/⅓ cup sultanas

30 g/1 oz hazelnuts, chopped

30 g/1 oz walnuts, chopped, plus 10–12 walnuts to decorate top of cake

Filling and topping

280 ml/½ pint/1¼ cups cream

170 g/6 oz dark cooking chocolate

Sieve the flour, bread soda, baking powder, cocoa and salt into a bowl. Add in the sugar, golden syrup, milk, oil and beaten egg. Beat at a low speed with an electric mixer; when smooth and well mixed, add the sultanas and chopped nuts.

Put the mixture into a well-greased 20 cm/8 inch tin/pan and cook in a preheated oven (160°C/325°F/Gas 3) for 40 minutes. When cooked, remove from the tin/pan and put on to a wire tray to cool.

For the filling: Bring the cream to the boil and remove from the heat. Add the broken chocolate pieces, whisk to melt, and allow to thicken. When the cake is cool, split and spread one-third of the chocolate on to the bottom half. Cover with the top half, and spread the remaining chocolate cream on top with a pallet knife. Decorate with whole walnuts.

For a special occasion: When you split the cake, sprinkle a few drops of rum on each half before you spread the filling.

CARAWAY SEED CAKE

225 g/8 oz/1 cup butter

280 g/10 oz/1⅓ cups caster sugar (US superfine sugar)

4 eggs, beaten

340 g/12 oz/3 cups flour, sieved

1½ tsp baking powder

1 tbsp caraway seeds

Beat the butter and the sugar in a large bowl until creamy and white. Add the eggs gradually, beating well between additions; add a little flour if the mixture shows any sign of curdling. Fold in the flour, the baking powder and the caraway seeds. Put into a greased 900 g/2 lb loaf tin/pan and bake in a preheated warm oven (160°C/ 325°F/Gas 3) for ¾ hour. Turn out on to a wire tray to cool.

This recipe brings back happy childhood memories to Sister Magdalena. Caraway seed cake always featured in the afternoon teas prepared by her late mother for the frequent Sunday visitors in her home in Castlelyons, Co. Cork.

SISTER BERNARD'S PORTER CAKE

110 g/4 oz/½ cup butter

170 g/6 oz/¾ cup brown sugar

225 g/8 oz/2 cups flour

½ tsp mixed spice (US cinnamon, clove, nutmeg)

2 eggs

½ tsp bread soda (US baking soda)

70 ml/2½ fl oz/⅓ cup porter

400 g/14 oz/2⅔ cups mixed dried fruit (US light and dark raisins, currants)

Grease a 900 g/2 lb loaf tin/pan and line with greaseproof paper (US parchment paper). Cream the butter and the sugar in a large bowl until pale and fluffy. Sieve the flour and the spice. Beat the eggs. Add the flour and the eggs alternately to the creamed butter and sugar. Dissolve the bread soda in the porter and add to the mixture. Finally, fold in the fruit, put into the prepared tin/pan and bake in a preheated oven (140°C/275°F/Gas 1½) for 1 hour, or until cake is done. Turn out on to a wire tray to cool.

BUCKFAST ABBEY HONEY CAKE

————————— ❧ —————————

110 g/4 oz/½ cup butter *or*
  margarine
225 g/8 oz/¾ cup Buckfast honey
2 eggs

225 g/8 oz/2 cups self-raising flour
pinch of salt
a little milk

Cream the butter and the honey in a large bowl. Beat the eggs well and add alternately with the sieved flour and salt. If the mixture is very stiff, add a little milk. Bake in a well-greased 17.8 cm/7 inch tin/pan for ¾–1 hour in a moderate oven (180°C/350°F/Gas 4).

The Benedictine Monks at Buckfast Abbey, mindful of the injunction of St Benedict,
'Then are they truly monks, if they live by the labour of their hands', practise a
number of crafts including bee-keeping. Brother Adam Kehrle, a world recognised
expert in the craft, has perfected the Buckfast queen. Buckfast honey is renowned
throughout the United Kingdom and much further afield.
This recipe was given to Kylemore Abbey by Father Bede Conlon of Buckfast Abbey.

PATRICIA'S STICKY GINGER BREAD

————————— ❧ —————————

110 g/4 oz/½ cup butter *or*
  margarine
225 g/8 oz/⅔ cup black treacle (US
  molasses)
55 g/2 oz/¼ cup brown sugar
225 g/8 oz/2 cups plain flour
4 level tsp ground ginger

½ tsp mixed spice (US cinnamon,
  clove, nutmeg)
½ tsp cinnamon
1 level tsp bread soda (US baking
  soda)
4 eggs, beaten
a little milk

Warm the butter, treacle, syrup and the sugar in a saucepan over a gentle heat. Sieve the flour, spices and the bread soda into a large bowl, and add the cooled treacle and syrup mixture. Add the beaten eggs with sufficient milk to make a thick pouring consistency. Mix well. Pour the mixture into a square or loaf tin/pan and bake in a preheated moderate oven (180°C/350°F/Gas 4) for 1–1¼ hours, or until firm to the touch.

CANADIAN BOILED FRUIT CAKE

450 g/1 lb/3 cups mixed dried fruit
  (US light and dark raisins,
  currants)
55 g/2 oz/½ cup walnuts *or* pecans,
  chopped

170 g/6 oz/1 cup sugar
110 g/4 oz/½ cup margarine
1 tsp bread soda (US baking soda)
225 ml/8 fl oz/1 cup water

Mix the ingredients listed above in a large saucepan, bring slowly to the boil and allow to boil for 5 minutes. Leave to stand overnight.

225 g/½ lb/2 cups sieved flour
2 eggs, beaten
2 tsp baking powder

1 tsp mixed spice (US cinnamon,
  clove, nutmeg)

Add the ingredients listed above, mix well and spoon the mixture into a greased and lined 20 cm/8 inch tin/pan and bake in a preheated warm oven (170°C/325°F/Gas 3) for 1 hour and 10 minutes. Cool for 15 minutes before removing from the tin/pan. Turn out on to a wire tray.

This recipe comes from Sister Benedict's Canadian grandmother.

LEMON MERINGUE PIE

Shortcrust Pastry

200 g/7 oz/1¾ cups flour
pinch of salt

110 g/4 oz/½ cup margarine
water to mix — about 7 tbsp

Filling

170 g/6 oz/¾ cup butter
4 egg yolks, whisked

110 g/4 oz/½ cup caster sugar (US
   superfine sugar)
juice and grated rind of 2 lemons

Meringue

4 egg whites

75 g/3 oz/⅓ cup caster sugar (US
   superfine sugar)

To make shortcrust pastry, sieve the flour and the salt into a large bowl. Cut the margarine into small knobs and rub into the flour until it is like fine breadcrumbs. Add the water and mix with a knife, gather into one piece by hand and knead lightly.

Line a 23 cm/9 inch flan dish (US pie dish) with the pastry and bake blind (page 131).

Melt the butter over a gentle heat, add the egg yolks, sugar, and the juice and rind of the lemons. Cook gently over a low heat until thickened; do not boil. Pour the lemon mixture on to the pastry.

Whisk the egg whites until stiff. Add the sugar and continue to whisk for a further few minutes. Spread the meringue over the lemon mixture ensuring that it comes well out to the sides. Bake for 15 minutes in a very cool oven (160°C/325°F/Gas 3) until the meringue is nicely browned. Allow the pie to settle before cutting.

MARY'S BAKEWELL

Shortcrust Pastry

170 g/6 oz/¾ cup flour
pinch of salt

110 g/4 oz/½ cup margarine
water to mix

Make the pastry as instructed above.

Madeira Mixture

110 g/4 oz/½ cup butter

110 g/4 oz/½ cup caster sugar (US superfine sugar)

140 g/5 oz/1¼ cups flour

1 level tsp baking powder

2 eggs

a little milk — 1–2 tbsp

Filling

2 good-sized cooking apples, peeled and thinly sliced

140 g/5 oz mincemeat — preferably homemade

55 g/2 oz/¼ cup sugar

Grease a 23 cm/9 inch flan dish (US pie dish) and line with the pastry, reserving a little for decoration. Trim the edges.

In a mixing bowl, cream the butter and the sugar until light and fluffy. Sieve the flour and the baking powder together. Beat the eggs lightly. Add the eggs and the flour alternately to the creamed butter and sugar, beating well between additions. Finally, add sufficient milk to make a spreadable mixture.

Put the apples on to the pastry and sprinkle with the sugar. Spread the mincemeat on top and then spread the cake mixture over the fruit, being careful to seal the sides.

Roll out the reserved pastry, together with the trimmings, and cut into strips about 0.6 cm/¼ inch wide. Place over the top of the cake at 2.5 cm/1 inch intervals, and cross over once to form a lattice pattern. Put into a preheated warm oven (160°C/325°F/Gas 3) for 1 hour. Remove carefully from the flan dish and cool on a wire tray.

KATE'S BAKEWELL

Shortbread

125 g/4½ oz/1 cup *plus* 2 tbsp flour

75 g/3 oz/6 tbsp butter

55 g/2 oz/¼ cup caster sugar (US superfine sugar)

Combine the ingredients until they form a stiff dough. (If using an electric whisk, use the paddle or spade, not the whisk.)

Sister Peter
playing her harp
against a scenic
backdrop

A view of the lake from the Abbey

Madeira Almond Mix

110 g/4 oz/½ cup butter

110 g/4 oz/½ cup caster sugar (US
   superfine sugar)

2 eggs

110 g/4 oz/1¼ cups ground
  almonds

110–170 g/4–6 oz/⅓–½ cup
  homemade raspberry *or*
  strawberry jam

Line the bottom of a 20 cm/8 inch flan dish (pie dish) with the shortbread, reserving a little to form a lattice on top.

In a mixing bowl, cream the butter and sugar together until light and creamy. Beat the eggs and add a little at a time, being careful not to let the mixture split. Next fold in the almonds. Spread the jam over the shortbread, but not quite out to the edge; leave about 1.2 cm/½ inch from the edge jam-free. Spread the almond mixture evenly all over, making sure it reaches the edge. Cut the remaining shortbread into narrow strips about 0.6 cm/¼ inch wide and arrange to form a lattice on top. Bake in a preheated cool oven (150°C/300°F/Gas 2) for 1 hour.

BLACKBERRY AND APPLE TART

—————————— ❧ ——————————

3 medium cooking apples, peeled,
  cored and sliced

140 g/5 oz/1 cup blackberries

75 g/3 oz/⅓ cup caster sugar (US
  superfine sugar)

Shortcrust Pastry

280 g/10 oz/2½ cups flour

170 g/6 oz/¾ cup butter *or*
  margarine

45 g/1½ oz/1½ tbsp caster sugar
  (US superfine sugar)

1 egg yolk

water to mix

Make the pastry as instructed on page 101.

Grease a 23 cm/9 inch tart plate (US shallow pie plate). Roll out half the pastry, line the plate and trim the edges. Spread the apples and blackberries on the pastry and sprinkle the sugar over. Brush the edges of the pastry with a little water. Roll out the remaining pastry and cover the tart. Seal the edges well and flute with a knife. Brush over with a little beaten egg yolk and bake in a preheated moderate oven (190°C/375°F/Gas 5) for 40–45 minutes until the pastry is brown. Sprinkle with some caster sugar and serve.

If you wish, you can stew the apples with the sugar and a tiny drop of water until partly cooked. When cool, add the blackberries and then put into the tart. This method requires a little less cooking time.

GOOSEBERRY TART

èa

280 g/10 oz/2½ cups flour
55 g/2 oz/½ cup icing sugar (US powdered sugar)
170 g/6 oz/¾ cup butter *or* margarine

1 egg yolk
a little water to mix
450 g/1 lb gooseberries, topped and tailed
110 g/4 oz/½ cup sugar

Sieve the flour and the icing sugar into a bowl, and rub in the margarine until it resembles fine breadcrumbs. Add the egg yolk and mix with a little water to a stiff dough. Turn out on to a floured board and divide the pastry in two. Grease a 23 cm/9 inch tart plate (US shallow pie plate), line with half the pastry and trim the edges. Spread the gooseberries evenly on to the pastry and sprinkle the sugar over the fruit. Brush the edges of the pastry with a little water. Roll out the remaining pastry and cover the tart, sealing the edges. Brush over with a little beaten egg and bake in a preheated moderate oven (190°C/375°F/Gas 5) for 40–45 minutes.

Gooseberry tart is always served in the monastery on 21 June, the feast of St Aloysius Gonzaga. Many years ago, on this date, a Nun was dying in great peace and contentment. All the Nuns were very sad and the dying Nun instructed them to be happy and to go and bake a nice pie for supper. They carried out her wishes, baked a gooseberry pie, and so it has been ever since.

MIXED FRUIT AND APPLE TART

❧

Pastry

280 g/10 oz/2½ cups flour

170 g/6 oz/¾ cup butter

55 g/2 oz/¼ cup caster sugar (US superfine sugar)

1 egg

a little water (about 2 tbsp)

Make the pastry as instructed on page 101.

Filling

170 g/6 oz/1 cup mixed dried fruit (US light and dark raisins, currants)

1 tbsp mincemeat

110 g/4 oz/½ cup brown sugar

2 tbsp alcohol *or* apple juice

3 medium cooking apples, peeled and sliced

Put the fruit, mincemeat, sugar and alcohol into a saucepan, bring to the boil and simmer very gently for 7–8 minutes. Remove from the heat and leave to cool.

Prepare the apples and cook to a pulp. Cool and add to the fruit mixture.

Line a 23 cm/9 inch shallow pie plate with half the pastry and spread the fruit evenly over. Dampen the edges and cover with the remaining pastry; seal and trim the edges. Brush over with beaten egg and bake in a preheated moderate oven (190°C/375°F/Gas 5) for 40 minutes.

The alcohol — sherry, whiskey or brandy — is not essential to this recipe, but it is strongly recommended and it does make a difference.

SISTER BENEDICT'S GINGER WAFER BISCUITS

❧

30 g/1 oz/2 tbsp butter

110 g/4 oz/4 tbsp golden syrup

110 g/4 oz/1 cup plain flour

1 tsp ground ginger

pinch of salt

15 g/½ oz/½ tbsp caster sugar (US superfine sugar)

¼ tsp bread soda (US baking soda)

a little milk

Melt the butter and the syrup together. Sieve the flour, ginger and the salt into a bowl. Add the sugar and stir in the melted butter and syrup. Add the bread soda, dissolved in a little milk, and mix well. Turn on to a floured board and roll out very thinly to less than 0.6 cm/¼ inch. Cut into rounds, place on a baking sheet and bake in a preheated moderate oven (180°C/350°F/Gas 4) for 15 minutes. Cool well before storing.

Ginger biscuits are always baked on the Feast of St Martin of Tours — a tradition from the days of Ypres.

PLAIN DIGESTIVE BISCUITS

170 g/6 oz/1½ cups wholemeal flour (US wholewheat flour)

30 g/1 oz/¼ cup white flour

30 g/1 oz/¼ cup oatmeal

2 tsp sugar

1 tsp baking powder

75 g/3 oz/6 tbsp butter *or* margarine

milk to bind

Mix all the dry ingredients together. Rub in the butter and add enough milk to bind and make a stiff dough. Turn out on to a floured board and roll out thinly. Cut into rounds using a 6.3 cm/2½ inch cutter. Put on a greased baking sheet and bake for approximately 20 minutes in a preheated cool oven (150°C/300°F/Gas 2). Be careful not to overbake; these biscuits should be pale when cooked. Cool on a wire tray.

OATCAKES

225 g/8 oz/2 cups oatmeal

110 g/4 oz/½ cup sugar

pinch of salt

1 tsp baking powder

55 g/2 oz dessicated coconut (US shredded coconut)

140 g/5 oz/1¼ cups white flour

240 g/9 oz/2¼ cups margarine

Mix all the dry ingredients together, melt the margarine, add to the dry ingredients and bind well. Roll out to 0.6 cm/¼ inch thick on a floured board and cut into rounds, using a 5 cm/2 inch cutter. Bake in a preheated very cool oven (140°C/275°F/Gas 1) for 15 minutes. If you want larger oatcakes, it is best to double the above recipe, roll out to 1.2 cm/½ inch thick and use a 7.6 cm/3 inch cutter; bake for 25 minutes.

SISTER JARLATH'S PANCAKES

225 g/½ lb/2 cups flour
½ tsp salt
1 tsp bread soda (US baking soda)
1 tbsp sugar

2 eggs
350 ml/12 fl oz/1½ cups sour milk
butter to fry
caster sugar (US superfine sugar)
and lemon wedges to serve

Sieve the flour, salt and the bread soda into a bowl, and add the sugar. Separate the yolks from the whites of the eggs, add the yolks to the flour and mix well. Gradually add sufficient sour milk to give the consistency of thick custard. Beat well and leave to stand for an hour or two. Beat the egg whites until stiff, add to the mixture and mix gently. Heat the butter on a frying pan, drop in spoonfuls of the batter and fry to a golden brown on each side. Sprinkle with the caster sugar and serve immediately with the wedges of lemon.

SALADS AND DRESSINGS

*I*n early times in the Monastery, summer days meant salad days. Salads then were a combination of summer vegetables — crisp fresh lettuce, sun-ripened tomatoes, scallions and farm-fresh hard-boiled eggs. Rarely served as a main course, this salad was, almost inevitably, accompanied by cold ham or, occasionally, cold chicken. Salad days were, in the long hot summers of yester-year, a real treat for the cooks, and greatly looked forward to. The coolness of the kitchen made a welcome change from the usual sweltering conditions when the ranges burned from early morning.

Nowadays, in common with the rest of us, the Nuns have salads all year round. They are many and varied, and we have selected a few favourites for inclusion.

SUMMER SALAD

2 medium tomatoes, quartered

1 small green pepper, deseeded and diced

2 spring onions, trimmed and chopped

2 sticks of celery, scrubbed and chopped

½ cucumber, washed and diced

1 carrot scraped and coarsely shredded

55 g/2 oz beansprouts, washed

French dressing — about 4 tbsp (page 117)

2 tsp chopped parsley

Combine all the vegetables together. Mix with the dressing just before serving and sprinkle with chopped parsley.

GREEN LEAF SALAD

———————— ❧ ————————

¼ head of iceberg lettuce

a few leaves of radicchio

2 spring onions, trimmed and chopped

½ cucumber, peeled and sliced

30 g/1 oz finely shredded white cabbage

10 sprigs of parsley, stalks removed

4 tbsp French dressing (page 117)

Wash and dry all the leaves. Coarsely shred the lettuce and break the radicchio leaves into small pieces. Combine all the ingredients together in a large bowl. Pour over the dressing just before serving and toss well.

SPINACH AND MUSHROOM SALAD

———————— ❧ ————————

225 g/½ lb fresh spinach

225 g/½ lb mushrooms

4 tbsp blue cheese dressing (pages 117–18)

Wash the spinach in salted water, remove any hard stalks, dry well and tear into small pieces. Wipe and slice the mushrooms, and mix with the spinach leaves. Cover, pour on the dressing just before serving and toss well.

CABBAGE AND APPLE SLAW

———————— ❧ ————————

¼ small Dutch cabbage, finely shredded

1 red apple, chopped

1 stick of celery, chopped

1 tbsp walnuts, chopped

1 tbsp sultanas

salt and pepper to taste

honey and yoghurt dressing (page 117)

Combine all the ingredients in a bowl and toss. Cover and refrigerate. Dress with the yoghurt and honey dressing before serving (omitting the dill for this particular salad).

The Drawing-room, often referred to as the Library, on a sunny summer's day

Sister Magdalena's Silver Jubilee cake, beautifully iced by herself for the occasion

CUCUMBER AND YOGHURT SALAD

———————— ❧ ————————

2 large cucumbers
280 ml/½ pint/1¼ cups natural
  yoghurt
2 tsp chopped mint

2 tsp lemon juice
1 tbsp chopped chives
salt and freshly ground black
  pepper

Peel and thinly slice the cucumber. Combine all the other ingredients, reserving a little of the chives to sprinkle on top. Check seasoning. Add the cucumber to the yoghurt mix. Sprinkle remaining chives on top. Cover and put into a fridge until ready to use.

TOMATO AND MOZZARELLA SALAD

———————— ❧ ————————

110 g/4 oz Mozzarella cheese
450 g/1 lb tomatoes
small bunch of fresh basil
120 ml/4 fl oz/½ cup olive oil

1 clove of garlic, crushed
salt and freshly ground black
  pepper

Cut the cheese into slivers and place in the centre of a flat dish. Slice the tomatoes and layer around the cheese, overlapping. Tear the basil and add to the olive oil with the garlic, salt and pepper. Before serving, pour a little of the dressing over the salad.

DOLORES'S ORANGE AND CRESS SALAD

———————— ❧ ————————

½ medium head of Chinese leaves
  (US Chinese cabbage)

1 bunch of watercress
2 oranges, peeled and segmented
  (page 131)

Oriental Dressing

1 tbsp tarragon vinegar
1 tbsp soy sauce

½ tbsp honey
150 ml/¼ pint/⅔ cup olive oil

1 tbsp orange juice

1 clove of garlic, peeled and crushed

salt and pepper

Wash, dry and shred the lettuce. Wash the watercress and remove any long stalks. Put the lettuce, orange and the watercress in a large bowl, toss, cover and chill until using. Mix all the ingredients for the dressing together. Pour a little over the salad before serving.

ORANGE, CHICKEN AND BEAN SPROUT SALAD

2 oranges

225 g/½ lb beansprouts

225 g/½ lb cooked chicken, cut into strips

1 tbsp pistachio nuts, roughly cut

1 tbsp chopped chives

Dressing

90 ml/3 fl oz/⅓ cup olive oil

juice of 1 orange

juice of ½ lemon

salt and freshly ground black pepper

Peel and segment the oranges (page 131). Wash the beansprouts, drain and pick over. Put into a bowl with the orange segments and the chicken. Refrigerate for 2 hours. Make the dressing by combining all the ingredients in a jar and shaking well. Before serving, add the nuts and the chives. Toss and sprinkle a little of the dressing over. Toss again. Serve the remaining dressing in a separate jug.

COCONUT RICE SALAD

225 g/½ lb/1 cup long grain rice

2 tbsp coconut cream

1 tbsp hazelnuts

½ cucumber

1 small pineapple

salt and pepper

coriander leaves to garnish

Cook the rice in plenty of boiling water and drain. Transfer to a bowl and stir in the cream coconut while the rice is still hot. Stir until melted. Chop the hazelnuts and cucumber, add to the rice and season. Peel, core and chop the pineapple into pea-sized cubes; add to the rice mixture. Cover and chill for 1–1½ hours. Transfer to serving bowls and garnish with coriander leaves.

SMOKED MACKEREL PÂTÉ

225 g/8 oz smoked mackerel
200 g/7 oz cream cheese
freshly ground black pepper

juice of 1 lemon
lemon wedges to garnish

Remove the skin and bone from the fish. Put into a food processor together with the cheese, pepper and the lemon juice. Blend to a smooth paste, transfer to a container, cover and refrigerate for several hours. Serve the pâté in individual ramekins, or any small dishes, garnish with slices of lemon and serve with a generous helping of any green salad.

POTTED SMOKED TROUT

140 g/5 oz smoked trout fillets
140 g/5 oz/⅔ cup butter, softened
140 g/5 oz cream cheese
1 tbsp lemon juice

1 tsp fresh fennel, finely chopped
salt and freshly ground black
  pepper
sprigs of fennel to garnish

Using a food processor, blend the trout, butter and the cream cheese, add the lemon juice, transfer to a bowl, mix in the fennel and season to taste. Put into a container, cover and refrigerate for several hours. Remove from the fridge 20–30 minutes before using. Spoon into individual ramekins and serve with a green leaf salad (page 110). Garnish with the sprigs of fennel.

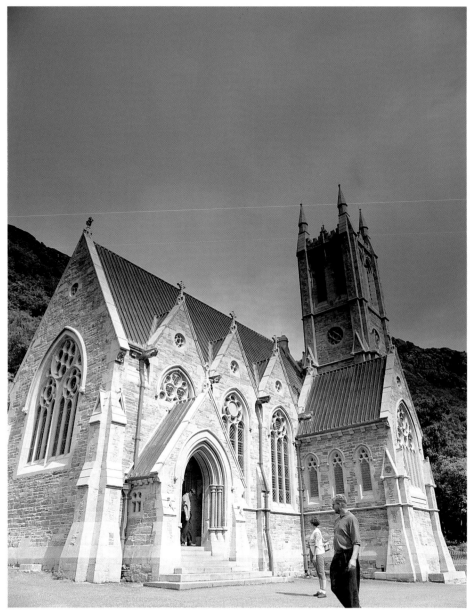

Visitors view the beautiful Gothic Church on a summer's day.

TUNA, APPLE AND CELERY SALAD

———————— ?♠ ————————

1 x 340 g/12 oz tin tuna fish
3 red apples, cored and diced
3 sticks of celery, washed and
  chopped

½ tbsp lemon juice
3 tbsp French dressing (page 117)
1 head of chicory, washed
2 tsp chopped parsley

Drain the tuna fish and flake. Combine the apples, celery and the lemon juice, mix in the flaked tuna. Pour on the French dressing and toss well. Arrange the chicory leaves (or any variety of lettuce) around a flat dish, pile the tuna mixture in the centre and sprinkle the parsley on top.

STUFFED SMOKED SALMON ROLLS

———————— ?♠ ————————

8 slices smoked salmon
170 g/6 oz smoked mackerel pâté
  (page 114)

lemon wedges to garnish
green salad of choice *or* assorted
  salads to serve

Place the smoked salmon slices between two sheets of greaseproof paper (US parchment paper) — you can do half at a time. Using a rolling pin, roll gently to stretch the slices. Remove the top sheet of greaseproof paper. Put the pâté into a forcing bag, and using a large plain nozzle, pipe a strip of pâté down the centre of each slice of salmon. Roll up the slices and tuck in the edges. Place the salmon on a flat dish, cover and put in a fridge for a few hours, or into a freezer for 15 minutes. Serve two salmon rolls per person, garnished with lemon wedges, and surrounded by salads of choice.

STUFFED EGGS

———————— ?♠ ————————

6 hard-boiled eggs, shelled
30 g/1 oz/2 tbsp softened butter
1½ tbsp mayonnaise
1 tbsp chopped parsley

1 tbsp minced ham (alternatively
  minced chicken, sardines, salmon
  or grated cheese)
salt and freshly ground black
  pepper

Cut the eggs in half lengthwise, remove the yolks, put into a bowl and pound or mash well. Add the butter, mayonnaise, some of the parsley and minced ham (or alternative), season and taste. Put the mixture into a forcing bag and pipe back into the egg whites. Sprinkle the remaining parsley on top. Serve 3 halves per person, surrounded by salads of choice.

KYLEMORE FRENCH DRESSING

425 ml/¾ pint/1¾ cups olive oil
150 ml/¼ pint/⅔ cup wine vinegar
1 tbsp wholegrain mustard
2 tsp honey

salt and freshly ground black pepper
1 clove of garlic, peeled and crushed

Put all the ingredients into a large, lidded jar. Shake vigorously. Use as needed, shaking well before use.

HONEY AND YOGHURT DRESSING

1 tbsp lemon juice
1 tbsp honey
280 ml/½ pint/1¼ cups natural yoghurt

1 clove of garlic, peeled and crushed
salt and freshly ground black pepper
1 tsp freshly chopped dill

Mix together the lemon and the honey, add the yoghurt, garlic, season to taste and finally add the dill. Store in a covered jar.

BLUE CHEESE DRESSING

85 g/3 oz blue cheese
1 clove of garlic, peeled and crushed
2 tsp lemon juice
70 ml/2½ fl oz/⅓ cup tarragon vinegar

2 tsp made mustard (US prepared mustard)
280 ml/½ pint/1¼ cups olive oil
salt and freshly ground black pepper

Blend the cheese, garlic, lemon juice, vinegar and the mustard in a food processor. Transfer to a bowl, and beat in the olive oil. Season to taste and store in a lidded jar. Shake well before using.

ORIENTAL DRESSING

1 tbsp tarragon vinegar

1 tbsp soy sauce

½ tbsp honey

150 ml/¼ pint/⅔ cup olive oil

1 tbsp orange juice

1 clove of garlic, peeled and crushed

salt and pepper

Put all the ingredients together in a bowl and stir to blend together. Pour over the salad.

MAYONNAISE

2 egg yolks

salt and pepper

½ tsp mustard

1 tsp caster sugar (US superfine sugar)

280 ml/½ pint/1¼ cups olive oil

1 tbsp vinegar

Put the egg yolks into a bowl with the salt, pepper, mustard and sugar, and mix well. Add the oil, drop by drop, whisking all the time. As the sauce thickens, you can add the oil a little more quickly. When all the oil has been added, thin down with the vinegar and check seasoning.

COCKTAIL SAUCE

To 280 ml/½ pint/1¼ cups mayonnaise (above) add:

2 tsp lemon juice

150 ml/¼ pint/⅔ cup cream, lightly whipped

3 tsp tomato purée

additional seasoning if required

PUDDINGS AND DESSERTS

---

*D*esserts have always been popular with the Community; they form an important, and much discussed, part of the midday meal.

The basis of today's selection of puddings and desserts is that which is produced and cultivated from within the Abbey — fruits from the garden and dairy produce from the farm. So the emphasis is on fruit tarts and pies, milk puddings and custards, and the lighter stewed fruits, compotes and yoghurts. But even here modern trends are apparent, and increasingly the option is to end a meal with fruit and a little cheese, in keeping with today's healthy eating habits.

SISTER MARIE BERNARD'S QUEEN OF PUDDINGS

---

280 ml/½ pint/1¼ cups cream
280 ml/½ pint/1¼ cups milk
55 g/2 oz/¼ cup caster sugar (US superfine sugar)

grated rind of 1 lemon
4 eggs, beaten
30 g/1 oz/½ cup breadcrumbs
2 tbsp raspberry jam

Meringue topping

2 egg whites

55 g/2 oz/¼ cup caster sugar

Put the cream, milk, sugar and lemon rind into a saucepan, and bring to boiling point. Whisk on to the beaten eggs. Stir in the breadcrumbs and leave to stand for 10 minutes. Ladle the mixture into a greased pie dish. Place in a bain marie (page 132) and bake at 160°C/325°F/Gas 3 for 25–35 minutes.

Remove from the oven and spread raspberry jam over the top. To make the meringue, whisk the egg whites until stiff, add the sugar and continue to whisk until the meringue forms peaks. Spread the meringue roughly over the pudding, and return to the oven until the meringue is nicely browned.

RESURRECTION PUDDING

—————————— ❧ ——————————

This is a very good way of using up leftover cake — sponge, madeira, chocolate etc.

Crumble the cake with the fingertips and soak in a good hot rich egg custard (page 53). Put into a serving dish, smooth over the top and allow to cool. Sprinkle with caster or icing sugar and serve with custard.

This recipe was resurrected by Sister Benedict from long-past records.

Today's alternative is to soak the cake in warm milk, and use as filling for a pie. Line a pie tin with good shortcrust pastry (pages 100–101). Spread the cake mixture evenly over the bottom, cover with pastry, brush over with beaten egg, and bake in a preheated moderate oven (180°C/350°F/Gas 4) for 20–30 minutes, until the pastry is cooked. Sprinkle with sugar and serve straight from the oven cut into small squares.

JOSEPHINE'S SEMOLINA SOUFFLÉ PUDDING

—————————— ❧ ——————————

575 ml/1 pint/2½ cups milk
a small pinch of salt
grated rind of 1 lemon
55 g/2 oz/⅓ cup semolina

3 eggs, separated
75 g/3 oz/⅓ cup sugar
cinnamon to sprinkle on top

Put the milk, salt and the lemon rind into a saucepan and bring to the boil. Remove from the heat, add the semolina and stir, return to the heat and cook gently until the semolina has thickened. Remove from the heat and allow to cool. Add the egg yolks and half the sugar to the semolina and mix well. Beat the egg whites until stiff, add the remaining sugar and continue to beat for a further few minutes. Fold the egg whites into the mixture, put into a glass bowl, sprinkle a little cinnamon on top and place in a fridge for several hours. Alternatively, you can bake in the oven (180°C/350°F/Gas 4) for 20 minutes, and serve hot. A fresh strawberry or raspberry sauce is very good with this dessert.

This pudding has to be made to be appreciated. It is so much nicer than one might think, glancing at the recipe.

LEMON RICE PUDDING

75 g/3 oz/½ cup pudding rice
575 ml/1 pint/2½ cups milk
grated rind of ½ lemon
55 g/2 oz/¼ cup sugar
30 g/1 oz/2 tbsp butter

2 eggs, separated
150 ml/¼ pint/⅔ cup cream
a little lemon curd (page 101)
chopped nuts, toasted

Rinse the rice under a cold tap and put into a pan with the milk and the lemon rind. Simmer gently until the rice is cooked. Remove the pan from the heat and add half the sugar, butter and the egg yolks. Mix well and leave until cold.

Beat the egg whites until stiff. Add the remaining sugar and beat for a further 2 minutes. Whip the cream until thick, mix the egg white and cream together and fold into the rice. Put the rice mixture into individual glass dishes. Beat a little drop of hot water into the lemon curd and put a spoonful over each dish. Sprinkle toasted nuts on top and serve chilled.

BREAD AND BUTTER PUDDING

45 g/1½ oz/3 tbsp butter
8 slices of white bread
55 g/2 oz/⅓ cup sultanas
575 ml/1 pint/2½ cups milk

3 eggs
45 g/1½ oz/2 tbsp sugar
vanilla flavouring
90 ml/3 fl oz/⅓ cup cream

Butter the bread and cut into fingers. Layer the bread into a greased pie dish with a little sprinkling of sultanas between the layers. Heat the milk. Beat the eggs, sugar and flavouring together, add the heated milk and stir until the sugar is dissolved. Beat in the cream, pour over the bread and allow to soak for at least half an hour. Bake in a preheated moderate oven (180°C/350°F/Gas 4) until set and browned on top, about 40 minutes.

An old-fashioned comforting pudding now making its return, this is very good hot, or indeed cold with a cup of tea.

SISTER BENEDICT'S BEESTINGS PUDDING

This is made using the milk from the second milking of a newly calved cow.

Take 2 cups of beestings, 1 cup of fresh milk, sugar to taste. Put into a pie dish and sprinkle with nutmeg. Bake in a moderate oven (180°C/350°F/ Gas 4) until set — about 30–40 minutes. At this point it looks exactly like baked custard.

This is a very old Abbey recipe. The milk from a cow that has just calved is full of nutrition, but is not widely used.

THE ABBOT'S CHOCOLATE CAKE

110 g/4 oz/1 cup margarine
340 g/12 oz/1½ cups sugar
55 g/2 oz/½ cup cocoa, blended
   with boiling water
4 egg yolks

200 g/7 oz/1¾ cups flour }
4 tsp baking powder } sieved
90 ml/3 fl oz/⅓ cup milk
whites of 4 eggs

Blend together the margarine, sugar and cocoa. Add the egg yolks and mix. Add alternately the flour, baking powder and milk, ending with flour. Beat the 4 egg whites until stiff and fold into the mixture. Bake in two 20 cm/ 8 inch tins/pans in a preheated moderate oven (180°C/350°F/Gas 4) for 30 minutes.

Sister Benedict picking berries for the kitchen

Icing

30 g/1 oz/2 tbsp butter

1 tbsp cocoa, blended with boiling
water

450 g/1 lb/3½ cups icing sugar (US
powdered sugar)

Melt the butter, beat in the other ingredients and mix well. When the cakes
are cold, spread a little of the icing on one half, sandwich together and
spread the remaining icing on top.

This recipe comes from Christopher Dillon, Abbot of Glenstal.

CHOCOLATE ROULADE

5 eggs, separated

140 g/5 oz/⅔ cup caster sugar (US
superfine sugar)

1 tsp instant coffee

140 g/5 oz plain chocolate (US
semi-sweet chocolate)

280 ml/½ pint/1¼ cups cream

2 tbsp rum

30 g/1 oz/¼ cup icing sugar (US
powdered sugar)

Place the egg yolks and the sugar in a mixing bowl. Beat until thick.
Dissolve the coffee in 1 tbsp hot water and place in a bowl with the
chocolate; place the bowl over a saucepan of warm water to melt the
chocolate. Beat the egg whites until stiff. Stir the chocolate and coffee into
the egg yolks and mix well. Gently fold in the egg whites. Put the mixture
into a lined Swiss roll pan (US jelly roll pan) and bake in a preheated warm
oven (160°C/325°F/Gas 3) for 15 minutes.

Meanwhile have ready a sheet of greaseproof paper (US parchment
paper), a little larger than the pan, generously sprinkled with caster sugar.
Remove from oven, turn the sponge out on to the greaseproof paper, trim off
the edges and roll up with the aid of the paper. Whip the cream and sweeten
with a little of the icing sugar. Add the rum. When the cake is cool, unroll,
spread with the rum cream, and roll again, this time without the paper.
Sprinkle with the remaining caster sugar and serve in fairly thick slices.

BLACKBERRY AND APPLE CRUNCH

900 g/2 lb cooking apples, peeled, cored and sliced

110 g/4 oz/½ cup caster sugar (US superfine sugar)

about 3 tbsp water

225 g/½ lb blackberries

225 g/½ lb/4 cups breadcrumbs, brown *or* white

110 g/4 oz/½ cup sugar

110 g/4 oz/½ cup butter and a little extra for the top

Put the apples in a saucepan with the caster sugar and the water, stew until half-cooked. Add the blackberries and continue to stew for a further 3–4 minutes. Put the fruit into a pie dish. Toast the breadcrumbs under a low grill until evenly browned, put into a bowl and add the sugar. Melt the butter and mix into the breadcrumbs. Sprinkle the crumbs over the fruit, dot with butter and bake in a preheated moderate oven (180°C/350°F/Gas 4) for 25 minutes. Serve hot or cold and with natural yoghurt or custard.

APPLE PONTARD

55 g/2 oz/½ cup flour

110 g/4 oz/½ cup caster sugar (US superfine sugar)

3 eggs

1 tbsp vegetable oil

280 ml/½ pint/1¼ cups milk

2 medium cooking apples, peeled, cored and sliced

Sieve the flour into a bowl, add the sugar and mix. Add the eggs and the oil and whisk for 3 minutes. Add the milk and mix to a smooth batter. Put the apples into a greased oven dish, and pour the batter over them. Bake in a preheated moderate oven (180°C/350°F/Gas 4) for 10 minutes, reduce the heat to a cool oven (150°C/300°F/Gas 2) and continue to cook for a further 40–45 minutes. Sprinkle with some caster sugar and cut into squares. This pudding is also excellent when cold.

Father Augustin Xavier-Costa has kindly given this recipe to Kylemore Abbey. It is one of the most popular in the refectory of the Benedictine Monastery of St Pierre de Solesmes, France.

RHUBARB AND BANANA CRUMBLE

———————— ?? ————————

900 g/2 lb rhubarb

sugar to sweeten rhubarb

450 g/1 lb bananas

½ tsp ginger

Crumble

225 g/½ lb/2¼ cups flour

55 g/2 oz/½ cup porridge oats (US
rolled oats)

30 g/1 oz/¼ cup chopped nuts

110 g/4 oz/½ cup brown sugar

¼ tsp baking powder

65 g/2½ oz/5 tbsp margarine

Stew the rhubarb in a little water and add sufficient sugar to sweeten. Peel and slice the bananas and add to the stewed rhubarb with the ginger.

Combine all the crumble ingredients except the margarine. Melt the margarine and add to the other ingredients. Put the rhubarb and banana mixture into a 23 cm/9 inch pie dish, cover the top with the crumble and dot with butter. Bake in a preheated moderate oven (180°C/350°F/Gas 4) until the crumble is nicely browned, about 30 minutes. Serve with home-made custard or natural yoghurt.

APPLE AND LEMON MOUSSE

———————— ?? ————————

675 g/1½ lb cooking apples, peeled,
cored and sliced

2 tbsp water

110 g/4 oz/½ cup sugar

grated rind and juice of 1 lemon

whites of 2 eggs

90 ml/3 fl oz/⅓ cup lightly
whipped cream

thin slices of lemon to decorate

Put the apples, water, half of the sugar, the lemon juice and rind into a saucepan, and cook slowly to a pulp. Put into a blender and blend until smooth. Leave to cool. Beat the egg whites until stiff, add the remaining sugar and continue to whisk for 1 minute. Fold first the cream into the purée and mix, followed by the egg whites. Put into individual glass bowls, and decorate with the slices of lemon. Refrigerate for an hour before serving.

Sister Ita and Mother Mechtilde

PEAR SORBET

——————— ?❧ ———————

150 ml/¼ pint/⅔ cup water
110 g/4 oz/½ cup sugar
3 pears

2 tbsp lemon juice
1 egg white
fresh lemon balm *or* sprigs of mint
  to garnish

Heat the water and the sugar in a saucepan. When it reaches boiling point, remove from the heat and allow to cool. Peel and core the pears, liquidise to a purée, add the lemon juice and mix well. Pour in the cold syrup and mix. Put into a freezer, and freeze for 2 hours until soft crystals have formed. Whisk the egg white until stiff. Remove the pear mix from the freezer and beat with a whisk until all the crystals have broken up. Fold in the egg white, return to the freezer and freeze until stiff — at this point the sorbet can either be put into individual glasses or frozen in one container. Remove from freezer 30–40 minutes before serving and put into a fridge. Serve in individual glasses, decorated with the lemon balm or sprigs of mint.

LEMON YOGHURT MUESLI

——————— ?❧ ———————

560 g/1¼ lb natural yoghurt
2 tbsp lemon curd (page 101)
3 tbsp porridge oats (US rolled
  oats)

thin slices of lemon
30 g/1 oz/¼ cup chopped nuts

Combine the yoghurt and lemon curd in a bowl and whisk together — if you first beat the lemon curd very slightly, it is easier to mix. Put into the fridge. About 10 minutes before serving, fold in the oatflakes. Serve in individual glasses, decorate with a slice of lemon in the centre of each glass and a border of nuts at the edge.

FRUIT SALAD

——————— ?❧ ———————

55 g/2 oz/¼ cup caster sugar (US
  superfine sugar)

280 ml/½ pint/1¼ cups water
juice of 1 lemon

2 oranges, peeled and segmented
  (page 131)

1 banana, peeled and sliced

170 g/6 oz green grapes, halved
  and pitted

1 eating apple, peeled, quartered
  and sliced thinly

1 pear, peeled, quartered and
  sliced

few slices of melon, peeled and cut
  in small slices (optional)

½ grapefruit, peeled and
  segmented (optional)

30 ml/1 fl oz/2 tbsp sherry

Put the sugar and the water into a saucepan, and heat to dissolve the sugar. Add the lemon juice and allow the syrup to cool. Combine all the fruits in a bowl, pour the syrup over, add the sherry, gently mix the fruits and liquid, cover and leave in a fridge for 3–4 hours before serving. Serve in a large glass bowl.

SPECIAL FRUIT SALAD

110 g/4 oz cherries, pitted

1 small punnet of strawberries,
  hulled and quartered

225 g/½ lb black grapes, pitted

1 peach, cut into thin slices

2 oranges, peeled and segmented
  (page 131)

½ measure Cointreau (US Orange
  Curaçao or Triple Sec)

Combine all the fruit in a bowl. Combine the Cointreau with any of the juices that come from the oranges when segmenting. Pour over the fruit. Cover and chill for 2 hours. Serve in a glass bowl.

CITRON GÂTEAU

450 g/1 lb cream cheese

150 ml/¼ pint/⅔ cup cream

225 g/½ lb/1 cup caster sugar (US
  superfine sugar)

grated rind of 3 lemons

6 leaves of gelatine

2 tbsp water

2 egg whites

fresh strawberries to decorate

Beat together the cream cheese, cream and half the sugar. Add the lemon rind. Dissolve the gelatine in cold water. Make a light syrup with the water and add the remaining sugar. Add the gelatine. Beat the egg whites until stiff, add the syrup beating continuously, and fold into the cheese mixture, mixing well. Pour the mixture into a lined mould, and leave in a fridge overnight. Turn out on to a large flat dish, decorate with halved strawberries and spread some additional strawberries around the dish.

From the Benedictine Monastery of Maredsous Abbey. Maredsous is one of the biggest Benedictine monasteries in Belgium, from which Glenstal is a foundation. This recipe is taken from their splendid cookbook, Recettes Gastronomiques, *in which all recipes are made from their own cheeses, with the kind permission of Abbot Nicholas.*

GOOSEBERRIES POACHED IN ELDERFLOWER JUICE

450 g/1 lb gooseberries, topped and tailed

110 g/4 oz/½ cup sugar

280 ml/½ pint/1¼ cups water

grated rind of 1 lemon

2 tbsp elderflower juice

Wash the gooseberries. Put the sugar, water and the lemon rind into a saucepan, bring to the boil. Reduce the heat, add the gooseberries and elderflower juice (fresh juice is best, of course); the syrup should almost cover the fruit. Cover and cook very slowly over a low heat until the fruit is soft but not broken. Cool and chill before serving in individual glass bowls.

✠

PAX

*The Benedictine Nuns at Kylemore Abbey
extend the 'Pax' — Peace of St Benedict — to all their readers.*

Cookery Terms

1. To bake blind
Baking the base of tarts or quiches without filling. Line a flan dish with pastry and trim the edges. Cut a round of greaseproof paper (US parchment paper) larger than the dish and place it on the pastry. Half fill with dried beans or peas, and bake at 200°C/400°F/Gas 6 for 15–20 minutes.

2. To make white sauce

Ingredients:
      55 g/2 oz/4 tbsp butter
      55 g/2 oz/½ cup flour
      575 ml/1 pint/2½ cups milk

Melt the butter in a saucepan, stir in the flour and cook for 2 minutes. Add the milk gradually and, continuing to whisk, bring to the boil until thickened.

3. To segment an orange
Peel the orange with a sharp knife and remove all the pith. Holding the fruit over a bowl, carefully cut each section free of membrane and lift out. The bowl will hold the escaping juices.

4. To skin and deseed a pepper
Put the pepper under a hot grill, turning as the skin blisters, but be careful not to burn. Peel off the skin; remove the seeds and membrane.

5. To skin and deseed a tomato
With a sharp knife, cut a cross at the base of the tomato. Dip the tomato into boiling water for a few seconds, remove from the water and the skin will peel off. To remove the seeds, cut the tomato crosswise and scoop out the seeds with a teaspoon.

6. BAIN MARIE
A pan containing water into which dishes are put to cook slowly in the oven so that curdling is avoided; or a double saucepan.

7. BOUQUET GARNI
A bunch of herbs tied together in muslin — parsley, thyme, bay leaf, peppercorns — and used for flavour in soups and stews.

8. INFUSE
A means of extracting flavour from herbs and spices, by pouring boiling water over and allowing to stand.

9. KNOCK BACK
The term used for kneading yeast breads after first rising.

10. LIAISON
Thickening for soups and stews made from flour, cornflour and egg yolks.

11. ROUX
Equal amounts of fat and flour cooked together to form a basis for thickening soups or stews.

12. SWEATING
Cooking vegetables very slowly in hot fat to extract their juices.

13. TRUSSING
Tying or skewering a bird into shape before cooking.

14. WHEY
The milk that remains liquid when the rest forms into curds — used in cheese-making.

Additional Note
All temperatures refer to domestic ovens and must be adjusted to suit each particular oven.

INDEX

Index

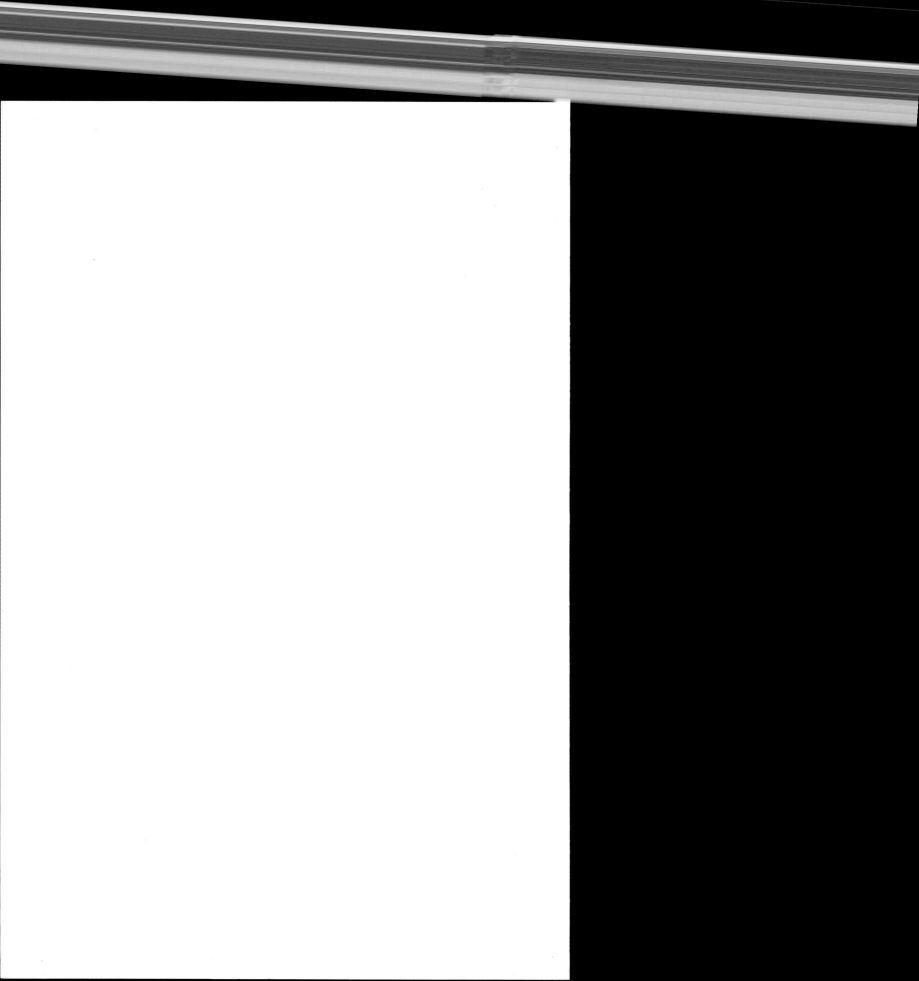